MEN'S 2025

FOOTBALL LEGENDS

PUBLISHED FOR THE USA IN 2024 BY WELBECK CHILDREN'S BOOKS
An imprint of Hachette Children's Group
Part of Hodder & Stoughton Limited
Carmelite House, 50 Victoria Embankment, London, EC4Y 0DZ
An Hachette UK Company
www.hachette.co.uk
www.hachettechildrens.co.uk

All statistical data and player heat maps provided by Opta, under license from Stats Perform.

STATS PERFORM

A catalogue record is available for this book from the British Library.

10 9 8 7 6 5 4 3 2 1
ISBN 978 1 8045 3733 6

Printed and bound in Dubai
Author: David Ballheimer
Senior Commissioning Editor: Suhel Ahmed
Design Manager: Matt Drew
Picture research: Paul Langan
Production: Melanie Robertson

PICTURE CREDITS
The publishers would like to thank the following sources for their kind permission to reproduce the pictures in this book.

GETTY IMAGES: AC Milan 51; Ion Alcoba/Quality Sport Images 56; Filippo Alfero/Juventus FC 102; Eric Alonso 27; Emilio Andreoli 20, 103; ANP 28; Franco Arland 61; Gonzalo Arroyo Moreno 48, 76; Marc Atkins 29; Robbie Jay Barratt/AMA 98; Lars Baron 57; James Baylis/AMA 108B; Giuseppe Bellini 17, 97; Berengui/DeFodi Images 8; John Berry 21, 89; Bagu Blanco/Pressinphoto/Icon Sport 10; Shaun Botterill 44; Stefan Brauer/DeFodi Images 106T; Megan Briggs 75; Clive Brunskill 12; David S. Bustamante/Soccrates 22, 66, 80; Pedro Castillo/Real Madrid 34; Jean Catuffe 16; Matteo Ciambelli/NurPhoto 68; Emmanuele Ciancaglini/Ciancaphoto Studio 70; Tim Clayton/Corbis 40; Gareth Copley 106B; Oscar Del Pozo/AFP 111T; Paul Ellis/AFP 85; Gualter Fatia 63; Baptiste Fernandez/Icon Sport 94; Johnny Fidelin/Icon Sport 43; Julian Finney 38; Stuart Franklin 91; Edith Geuppert/GES Sportfoto 39; James Gill/Danehouse 83; Alex Gottschalk/DeFodi Images 33, 60; Stefano Guidi 101; Lionel Hahn 108T; Matthias Hangst 54; Alexander Hassenstein 95; Mike Hewitt 59, 110B; Elie Hokayem/Saudi Pro League 19; Mario Hommes/DeFodi Images 50, 79; Image Photo Agency 108B; Catherine Ivill 11; Fareed Kotb/Anadolu 49; Roland Krivec/DeFodi Images 30; Maurizio Lagana 110T; Christian Liewig/Corbis 100; Alex Livesey 64, 69, 90; Marco Luzzani 65, 73; Stuart MacFarlane/Arsenal FC 53, 107T; Giuseppe Maffia/NurPhoto 55; Manchester City FC 109T; Angel Martinez 24, 26, 62; Clive Mason 105; Matt McNulty/Manchester City FC 35; Mattia Ozbot/Inter 23; Minas Panagiotakis 36; Alex Pantling 41; Andrew Powell/Liverpool FC 7, 25; Pressinphoto/Icon Sport 46; David Price/Arsenal FC 52; Joe Prior/Visionhaus 15; ProShots 111B; Quality Sport Images 88; Manuel Queimadelos/Quality Sport Images 45; Michael Regan 78, 86, 107B; Pedro Salado/Quality Sport Images 14; Fran Santiago 72, 87; Oli Scarff/AFP 5; Silas Schueller/DeFodi Images 71; Juan Manuel Serrano Arce 13; Justin Setterfield 93; Alexandre Simoes/Borussia Dortmund 18, 37; Diego Souto/Quality Sport Images 96; Boris Streubel 74, 92; VI Images 82; Pedro Vilela 77; Visionhaus 9, 31, 42, 47, 67, 81; George Wood 99

Every effort has been made to acknowledge correctly and contact the source and/or copyright holder of each picture; any unintentional errors or omissions will be corrected in future editions of this book.

All facts and stats correct as of June 2024

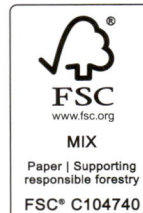

MEN'S 2025 FOOTBALL LEGENDS

STATS • PROFILES • TOP PLAYERS

WELBECK
CHILDREN'S BOOKS

CONTENTS

HOW TO USE THIS BOOK

Welcome to *Men's Football Legends 2025* — the exciting book packed with the performance stats of the biggest stars in the world of football today! We have chosen more than 100 players and managers who are superstars in the world's top five leagues: the Bundesliga in Germany, La Liga in Spain, France's Ligue 1, the Italian Serie A, and the English Premier League. The players are either playing in or have spent the majority of their careers up until the 2023/24 season operating in these top leagues.

You can use this book to work out who you think the best performers are by comparing the statistical data of today's finest defenders, midfielders, forwards, goalkeepers and managers.

The types of stats featured for each position vary, because each position performs a specific role on the field. For example, a defender's main job is to stop the opposition from scoring, so the stats focus mainly on this part of that player's game. Likewise, a striker's tackling is not as relevant as the player's goal or assists totals. What you will find for all the players is the heat map, which shows how much of the pitch a player covers and which areas he focuses his play in or, with goalkeepers, whether their strengths lie in the six-yard box or playing as sweeper keepers, who are comfortable all around the penalty area.

The stats span a player's career to date, for the most part playing for teams belonging to one of the top five European leagues. The figures have been collected from domestic league and European match appearances only, and exclude data from domestic cup, super cups or international games. This narrow data pool means that the information is instantly comparable so you can decide for yourself who truly deserves to be known as a living legend of the beautiful game.

DEFENDERS

There are different types of defenders. They cover a range of positions and have different skills. The centre-backs are the big defenders in the middle who mark the opposition strikers. Full-backs operate out wide: they are quick, agile and try to stop wide attackers from crossing balls into the box. Wing-backs play out wide, too, in front of the centre-backs, but also make attacking runs when they have the chance. Finally, the sweeper is the spare defender who is positioned behind the centre-half, ready to help the back four deal with any danger.

WHAT DO THESE STATS MEAN?

AERIAL DUELS WON
75%
This is the percentage of headers a defender has won in his own penalty area, to interrupt an opposition attack.

INTERCEPTIONS
This is the number of times a defender has successfully stopped an attack without needing to make a tackle.

BLOCKS
A shot that is intercepted by a defender - preventing his keeper from having to make a save - counts as a block.

KEY PASSES/PASS COMPLETION
A key pass is one that results in an attacking opportunity. Pass completion indicates as a percentage the player's passing accuracy.

CLEARANCES
An attack successfully foiled, either by kicking or heading the ball away from danger, is regarded as a clearance.

TACKLES
This is the number of times a defender has challenged and dispossessed the opposition without committing a foul.

Did you know?

For about 40 years from the late 19th century, the most common formation was 2–3–5. It featured only two defenders (right-back and left-back), while the centre-half played in midfield. There were five forwards.

4

NATIONALITY
Austrian

CURRENT CLUB
Real Madrid

DAVID ALABA

Although his best position is left-back, David Alaba's strength is his versatility. Superb with his positioning and reading of the game, his pace and athleticism also allow him to snuff out attacks before they have begun.

DATE OF BIRTH	24/06/1992
POSITION	LEFT-BACK
HEIGHT	1.80 M
PRO DEBUT	2007
PREFERRED FOOT	LEFT

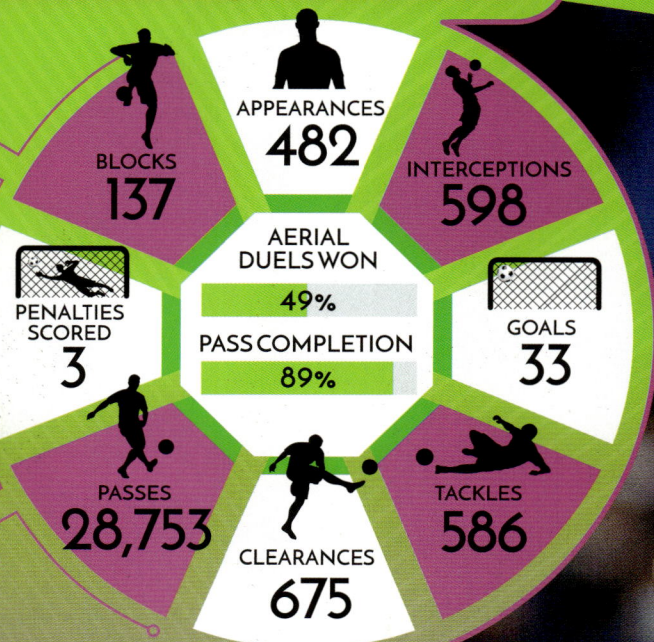

BLOCKS
137

APPEARANCES
482

INTERCEPTIONS
598

AERIAL DUELS WON
49%

PASS COMPLETION
89%

PENALTIES SCORED
3

GOALS
33

PASSES
28,753

CLEARANCES
675

TACKLES
586

MAJOR CLUB HONOURS

⚽ La Liga: 2022, runner-up 2023, 2024 ⚽ Bundesliga: 2010, 2013—2021 (all B. Munich.) ⚽ UEFA Champions League.: 2013, 2020 (all B. Munich), 2022, 2024 ⚽ FIFA Club World Cup: 2013, 2020 (all B. Munich), 2022 ⚽ UEFA Super Cup: 2022 ⚽ Copa del Rey: 2023

INTERNATIONAL HONOURS

⚽ None to date

ACTIVITY AREAS

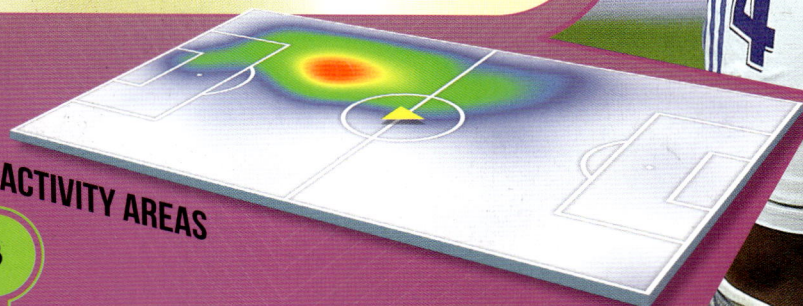

8

TRENT ALEXANDER-ARNOLD

Counted among the world's best overlapping defenders, Trent Alexander-Arnold plays at right-back or right wing-back. He is fast, tackles superbly and is capable of whipping in accurate crosses that strikers love to feast on!

NATIONALITY
English

CURRENT CLUB
Liverpool

66

DATE OF BIRTH	07/10/1998
POSITION	FULL-BACK
HEIGHT	1.75 M
PRO DEBUT	2016
PREFERRED FOOT	RIGHT

BLOCKS
36

APPEARANCES
283

INTERCEPTIONS
355

PENALTIES SCORED
0

AERIAL DUELS WON
39%

PASS COMPLETION
78%

GOALS
17

PASSES
17,187

CLEARANCES
405

TACKLES
462

MAJOR CLUB HONOURS
⚽ Premier League: 2020 ⚽ UEFA Champions League: 2019
⚽ UEFA Champions League: runner-up 2018, runner-up 2022
⚽ FIFA Club World Cup: 2019 ⚽ FA Cup 2022

INTERNATIONAL HONOURS
⚽ UEFA Nations League: third place 2019
⚽ UEFA European Championship: runner-up 2024

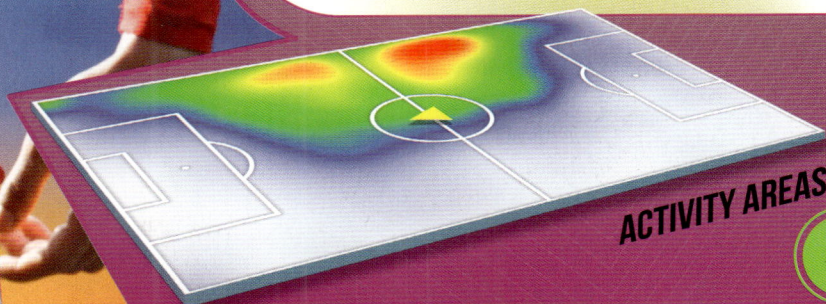

ACTIVITY AREAS

3

NATIONALITY
Spanish

CURRENT CLUB
Atlético Madrid

CÉSAR AZPILICUETA

Right-back César Azpilicueta is a natural leader, who can play anywhere on the pitch. He is excellent at using his positional sense to snuff out danger and frequently starts counter-attacks with a great right foot.

DATE OF BIRTH	28/08/1989
POSITION	FULL-BACK
HEIGHT	1.78 M
PRO DEBUT	2006
PREFERRED FOOT	RIGHT

BLOCKS
211

APPEARANCES
618

INTERCEPTIONS
1,098

AERIAL DUELS WON
57%

PASS COMPLETION
82%

PENALTIES SCORED
0

GOALS
15

PASSES
30,339

CLEARANCES
1,873

TACKLES
1,571

MAJOR CLUB HONOURS
⚽ Premier League: 2015, 2017 (Chelsea) ⚽ UEFA Champions League: 2021 (Chelsea) ⚽ UEFA Europa League: 2013, 2019 (all Chelsea) ⚽ FIFA Club World Cup: 2021, runner-up 2012 (Chelsea) ⚽ UEFA Super Cup: 2021 (Chelsea)

INTERNATIONAL HONOURS
⚽ UEFA Nations League: runner-up 2021
⚽ FIFA Confederations Cup: runner-up 2013

ACTIVITY AREAS

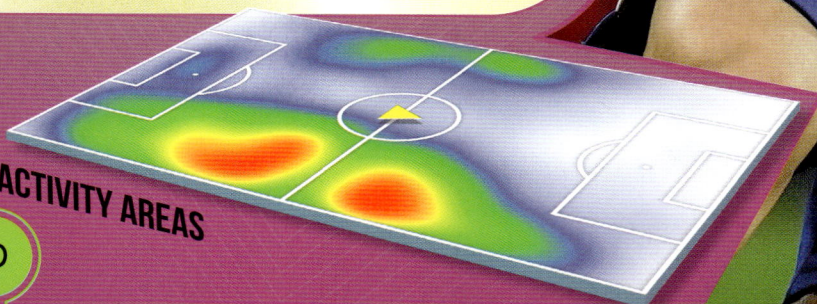

RÚBEN DIAS

Rúben Dias plays mainly on the left side of central defence, but is comfortable anywhere along the back line. He excels at winning challenges in the air and on the ground, making interceptions and delivering great passes with both feet.

NATIONALITY
Portuguese

CURRENT CLUB
Manchester City

3

DATE OF BIRTH	14/05/1997
POSITION	CENTRAL
HEIGHT	1.87 M
PRO DEBUT	2015
PREFERRED FOOT	RIGHT

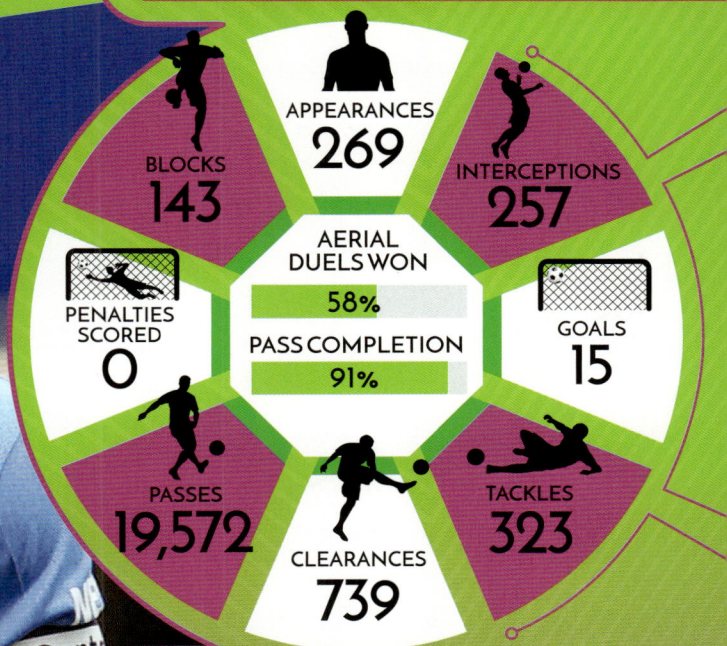

BLOCKS
143

APPEARANCES
269

INTERCEPTIONS
257

AERIAL DUELS WON
58%

PENALTIES SCORED
0

PASS COMPLETION
91%

GOALS
15

PASSES
19,572

CLEARANCES
739

TACKLES
323

MAJOR CLUB HONOURS

- ⚽ Premier League: 2021, 2022, 2023, 2024
- ⚽ UEFA Champions League: runner-up 2021, 2023
- ⚽ Portuguese Premier Liga: 2019 (Benfica)
- ⚽ FA Cup: 2023

INTERNATIONAL HONOURS

- ⚽ UEFA Nations League: 2019

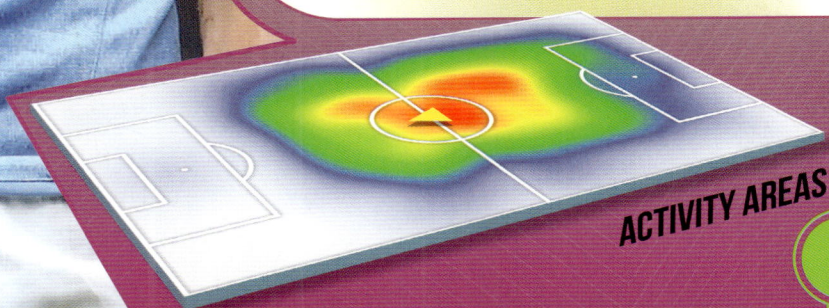

ACTIVITY AREAS

4

NATIONALITY
Dutch

CURRENT CLUB
Liverpool

VIRGIL VAN DIJK

Virgil van Dijk has returned to the form he showed before his 2020 knee injury. Good with either foot, he is a great tackler, a superb leader, wins headers in both penalty boxes and reads the game excellently.

DATE OF BIRTH	08/07/1991
POSITION	CENTRAL
HEIGHT	1.95 M
PRO DEBUT	2011
PREFERRED FOOT	RIGHT

BLOCKS
209

APPEARANCES
394*

INTERCEPTIONS
592

AERIAL DUELS WON
75%

PENALTIES SCORED
0

PASS COMPLETION
88%

GOALS
33

PASSES
25,603

CLEARANCES
2,151

TACKLES
445

*Excludes data from Scottish Premiership

MAJOR CLUB HONOURS

⚽ Premier League: 2020 ⚽ Scottish Premiership: 2014, 2015 (Celtic) ⚽ UEFA Champions League: 2019, runner-up 2018, runner-up 2022 ⚽ FIFA Club World Cup: 2019 ⚽ FA Cup: 2022

INTERNATIONAL HONOURS

⚽ UEFA Nations League: runner-up 2019

ACTIVITY AREAS

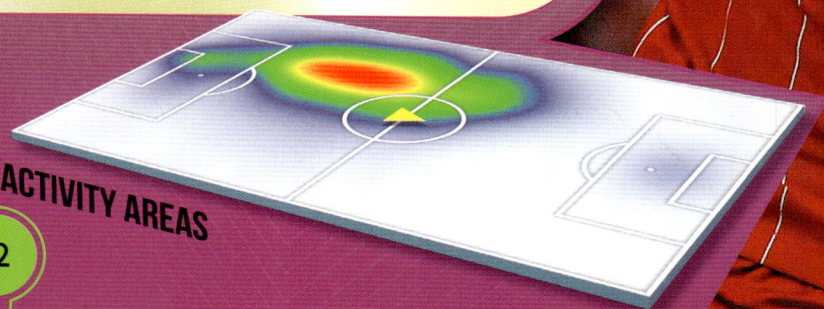

JEREMIE FRIMPONG

Jeremie Frimpong is as comfortable in midfield as he is a wing-back and fits perfectly in both roles. He uses his great pace and passing ability in attacking situations, but has the technical skills to be a great defender.

NATIONALITY
Dutch

CURRENT CLUB
Bayer Leverkusen

DATE OF BIRTH	10/12/2000
POSITION	RIGHT WING-BACK
HEIGHT	1.72 M
PRO DEBUT	2019
PREFERRED FOOT	RIGHT

BLOCKS
13

APPEARANCES
138*

INTERCEPTIONS
61

PENALTIES SCORED
0

AERIAL DUELS WON
39%

PASS COMPLETION
82%

GOALS
22

PASSES
4,023

CLEARANCES
116

TACKLES
159

*Excludes data from Scottish Premiership

MAJOR CLUB HONOURS
⚽ Bundesliga: 2024 ⚽ UEFA Europa League: runner-up 2024 ⚽ Scottish Premiership: 2020 (Celtic) ⚽ Scottish Cup: 2020

INTERNATIONAL HONOURS
⚽ None to date

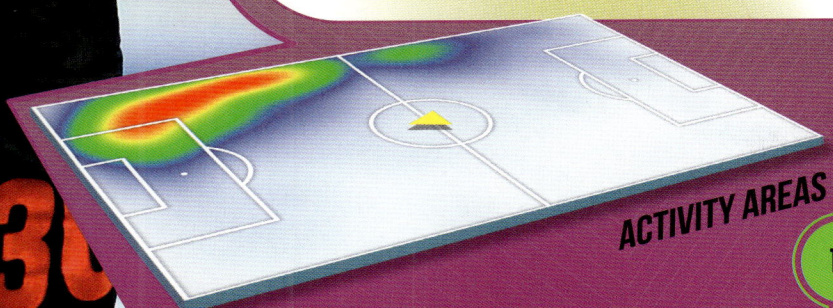

ACTIVITY AREAS

2

NATIONALITY
Uruguayan

CURRENT CLUB
Atlético Madrid

JOSÉ GIMÉNEZ

The Uruguayan is a tough-tackling centre-back who is quick off the mark and difficult to knock off the ball. He made his international debut when he was just 19 and has also thrived at club level since joining Atlético Madrid in 2013.

DATE OF BIRTH	20/01/1995
POSITION	CENTRAL
HEIGHT	1.85 M
PRO DEBUT	2012
PREFERRED FOOT	RIGHT

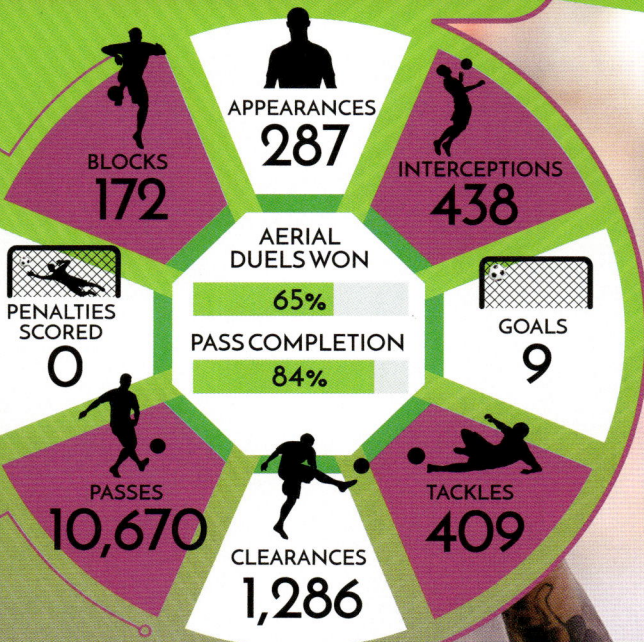

BLOCKS
172

APPEARANCES
287

INTERCEPTIONS
438

AERIAL DUELS WON
65%

PASS COMPLETION
84%

PENALTIES SCORED
0

GOALS
9

PASSES
10,670

TACKLES
409

CLEARANCES
1,286

MAJOR CLUB HONOURS
- La Liga: 2014, 2021
- UEFA Europa League: 2018
- UEFA Super Cup: 2018
- UEFA Champions League: runner-up 2014, 2016

INTERNATIONAL HONOURS
- FIFA U-20 World Cup: runner-up 2013
- China Cup: 2018, 2019

ACTIVITY AREAS

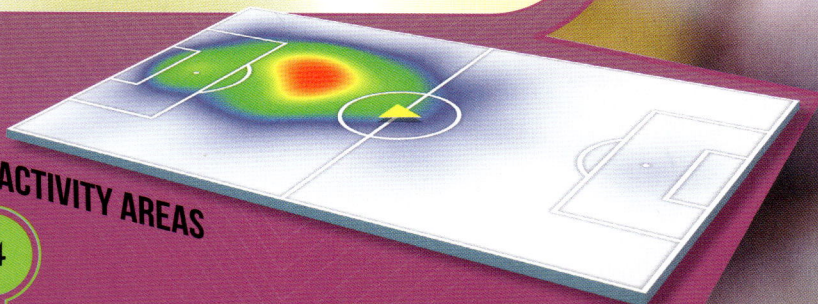

JOŠKO GVARDIOL

The 22-year-old Joško Gvardiol has emerged as one of Europe's most talented defenders. His ability to defend in one-on-one situations, make key interceptions and tackles are matched by his skills when he turns defence into attack.

NATIONALITY
Croatian

CURRENT CLUB
Manchester City

24

DATE OF BIRTH	23/01/2002
POSITION	CENTRAL
HEIGHT	1.85 M
PRO DEBUT	2019
PREFERRED FOOT	LEFT

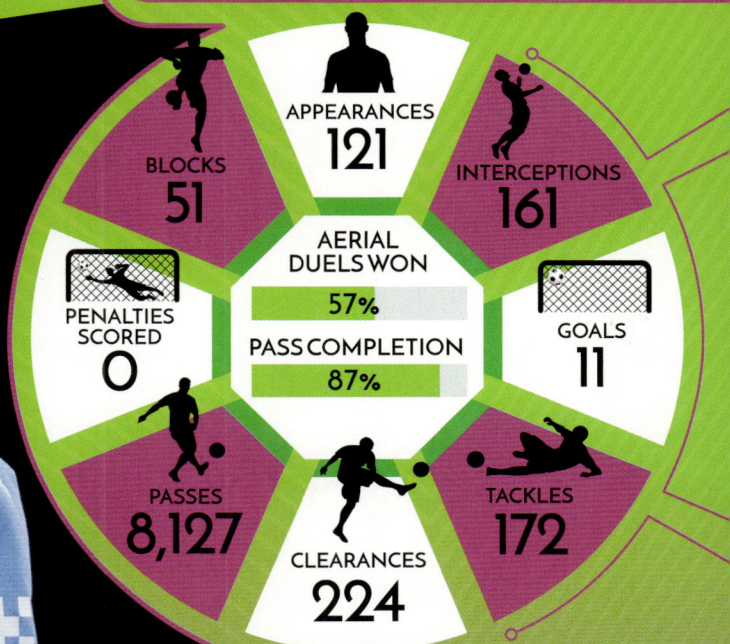

BLOCKS
51

APPEARANCES
121

INTERCEPTIONS
161

PENALTIES SCORED
0

AERIAL DUELS WON
57%

PASS COMPLETION
87%

GOALS
11

PASSES
8,127

CLEARANCES
224

TACKLES
172

MAJOR CLUB HONOURS
- Premier League: 2024
- DFB Pokal: 2022, 2023 (RP Leipzig)
- UEFA Super Cup: 2023
- FIFA Club World Cup: 2023

INTERNATIONAL HONOURS
- FIFA World Cup: third place 2022

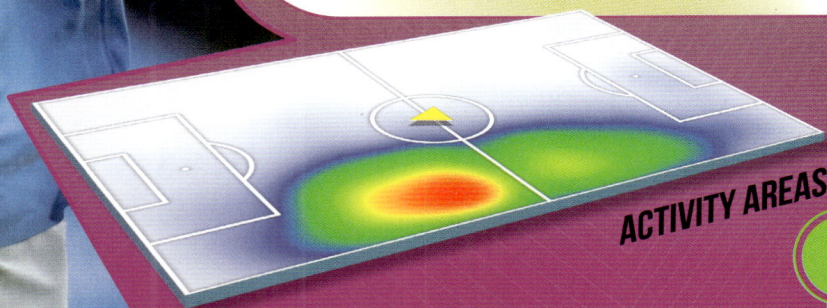

ACTIVITY AREAS

ACHRAF HAKIMI

Born in Spain to Moroccan parents, Ashraf Hakimi has played and enjoyed success at some of Europe's top clubs. Known for his blistering pace and keen attacking instincts, he can play as a midfielder or wing-back, and can even score and create goals.

NATIONALITY
Moroccan

CURRENT CLUB
Paris Saint-Germain

2

DATE OF BIRTH	04/11/1998
POSITION	RIGHT-BACK
HEIGHT	1.81 M
PRO DEBUT	2016
PREFERRED FOOT	RIGHT

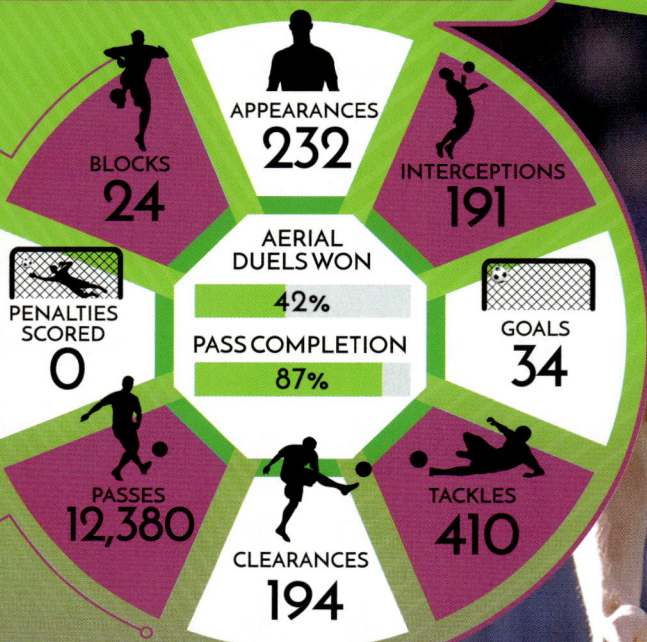

APPEARANCES
232

BLOCKS
24

INTERCEPTIONS
191

AERIAL DUELS WON
42%

PASS COMPLETION
87%

PENALTIES SCORED
0

GOALS
34

PASSES
12,380

TACKLES
410

CLEARANCES
194

MAJOR CLUB HONOURS
⚽ Ligue 1: 2022, 2023, 2024 ⚽ Serie A: 2021 (Inter Milan) ⚽ UEFA Champions League: 2018 (R. Madrid) ⚽ FIFA World Club Cup: 2017 (R. Madrid) ⚽ Coupe de France: 2024

INTERNATIONAL HONOURS
⚽ None to date

ACTIVITY AREAS

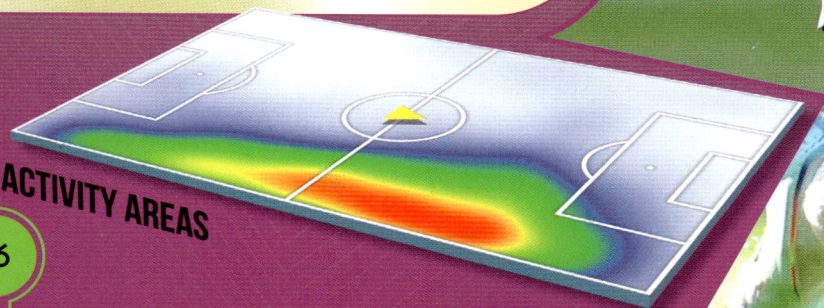

THEO HERNÁNDEZ

Known more for his attacking qualities than his defensive work, Theo Hernández (younger brother of Lucas) is a footballer that is blessed with great pace, can dribble rapidly with the ball at his feet, and possesses the capability to get into goalscoring positions. He has become a fan favourite at AC Milan.

NATIONALITY
French

CURRENT CLUB
AC Milan

19

DATE OF BIRTH	06/10/1997
POSITION	LEFT-BACK
HEIGHT	1.84 M
PRO DEBUT	2015
PREFERRED FOOT	LEFT

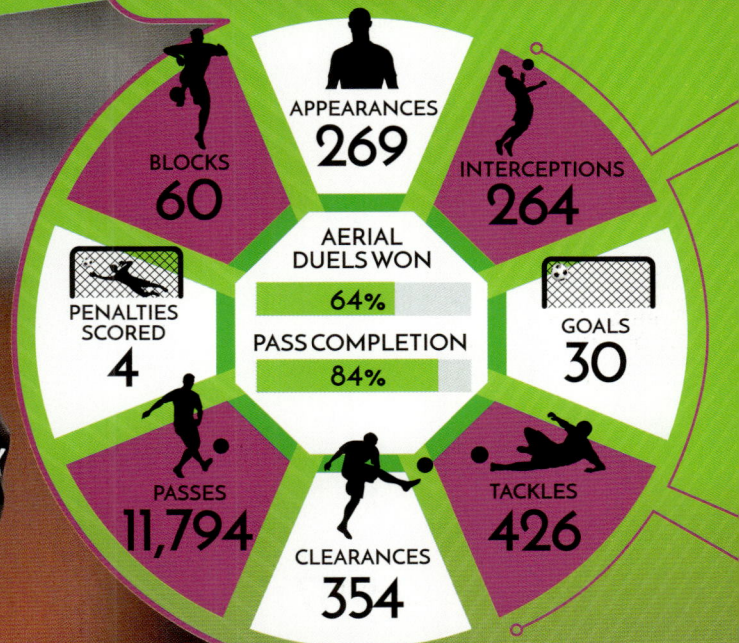

APPEARANCES
269

BLOCKS
60

INTERCEPTIONS
264

AERIAL DUELS WON
64%

PASS COMPLETION
84%

PENALTIES SCORED
4

GOALS
30

PASSES
11,794

CLEARANCES
354

TACKLES
426

MAJOR CLUB HONOURS
⚽ Serie A: 2022 ⚽ UEFA Champions League: 2018 (R. Madrid) ⚽ FIFA World Club Cup: 2017 (R. Madrid) ⚽ UEFA Super Cup 2017 (R. Madrid)

INTERNATIONAL HONOURS
⚽ FIFA World Cup: runner-up 2022
⚽ UEFA Nations League: 2021

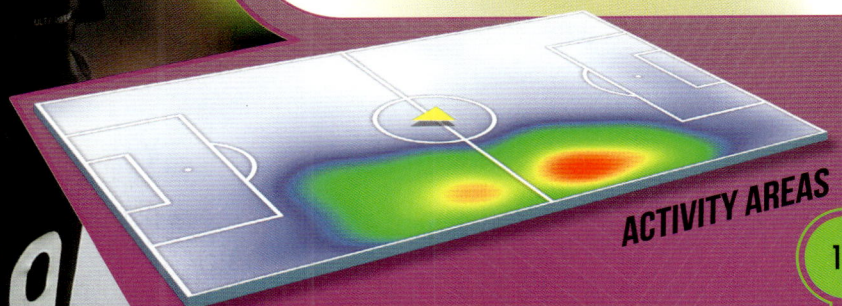

ACTIVITY AREAS

MATS HUMMELS

The German is regarded as one of the best ball-playing defenders on the planet. Hummels can physically tussle with the strongest of forwards, but it is his ability to stride forward and set up attacks with his fine passing that sets him apart.

NATIONALITY
German

CURRENT CLUB
TBC

DATE OF BIRTH	16/12/1988
POSITION	CENTRAL
HEIGHT	1.91 M
PRO DEBUT	2006
PREFERRED FOOT	RIGHT

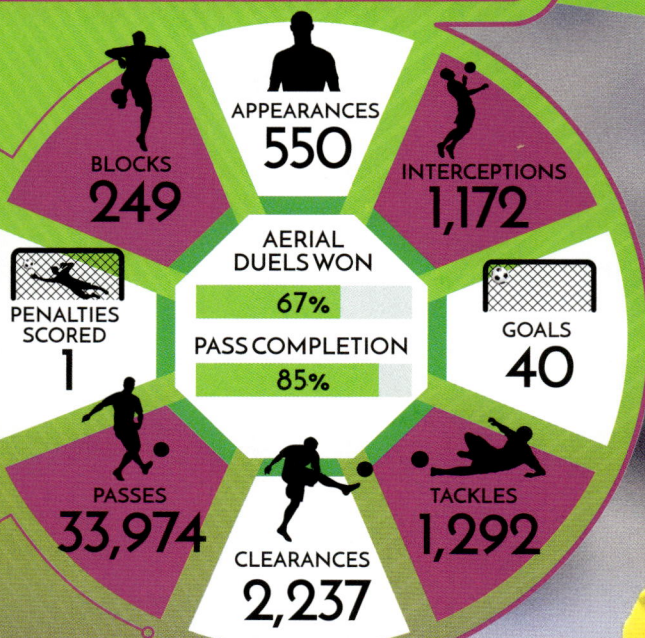

BLOCKS
249

APPEARANCES
550

INTERCEPTIONS
1,172

PENALTIES SCORED
1

AERIAL DUELS WON
67%

PASS COMPLETION
85%

GOALS
40

PASSES
33,974

CLEARANCES
2,237

TACKLES
1,292

MAJOR CLUB HONOURS
⚽ Bundesliga: 2011*, 2012* (B. Dortmund*), 2017, 2018 (all B. Munich), 2019 (B. Munich), runner-up 2023 (B. Dortmund) ⚽ DFB-Pokal: 2012 (B. Dortmund), 2019 (B. Munich), 2021 (B. Dortmund) ⚽ UEFA Champions League: runner-up 2013, runner-up 2024 (all B. Dortmund)

INTERNATIONAL HONOURS
⚽ FIFA World Cup: 2014

ACTIVITY AREAS

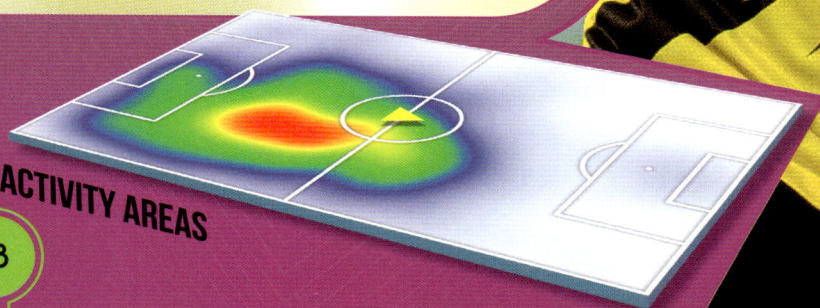

AYMERIC LAPORTE

Aymeric Laporte was among Europe's best defenders before moving to the Saudi Pro League in 2023. Very strong, he is a powerful tackler, excellent in the air and a good organiser at the back. Laporte can also start attacks with his precise passing out of defence.

NATIONALITY
Spanish

CURRENT CLUB
Al Nassr

27

DATE OF BIRTH	27/05/1994
POSITION	CENTRAL
HEIGHT	1.89 M
PRO DEBUT	2011
PREFERRED FOOT	LEFT

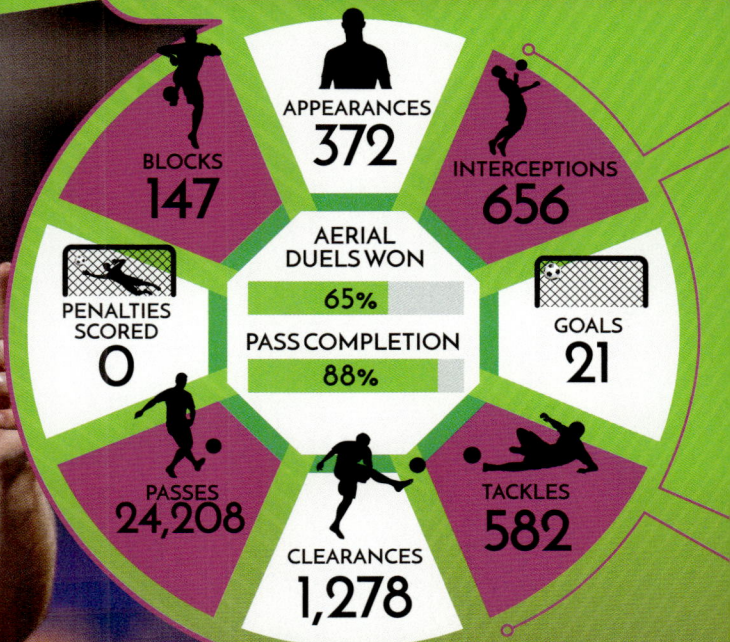

BLOCKS
147

APPEARANCES
372

INTERCEPTIONS
656

PENALTIES SCORED
0

AERIAL DUELS WON
65%

PASS COMPLETION
88%

GOALS
21

PASSES
24,208

CLEARANCES
1,278

TACKLES
582

MAJOR CLUB HONOURS
⚽ Premier League: 2018, 2019, 2021, 2022, 2023 (all Man. City) ⚽ UEFA Champions League: runner-up 2021, 2023 (all Man. City) ⚽ FA Cup: 2019, 2023 (all Man. City)

INTERNATIONAL HONOURS
⚽ UEFA Nations League: runner-up 2021, 2023
⚽ UEFA European U-19 Championship: runner-up 2013 (France)
⚽ UEFA European Championship: 2024

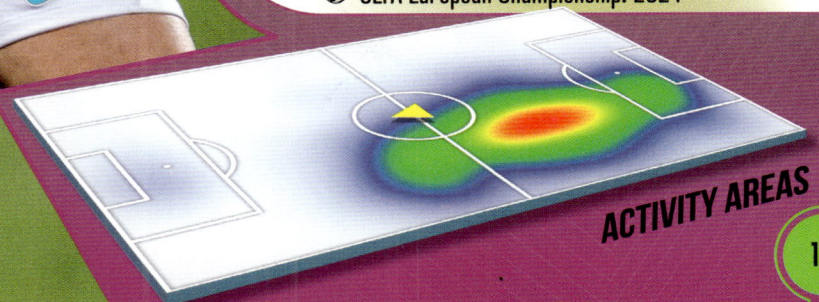

ACTIVITY AREAS

19

22

NATIONALITY
Italian

CURRENT CLUB
Napoli

GIOVANNI DI LORENZO

Although he began his professional career as an attacking player, Giovanni di Lorenzo is now an excellent defender, normally at right-back, but he can play in the middle too. He has a solid tackling technique, is physically strong and possesses good aerial ability.

DATE OF BIRTH	04/08/1993
POSITION	RIGHT-BACK
HEIGHT	1.83 M
PRO DEBUT	2010
PREFERRED FOOT	BOTH

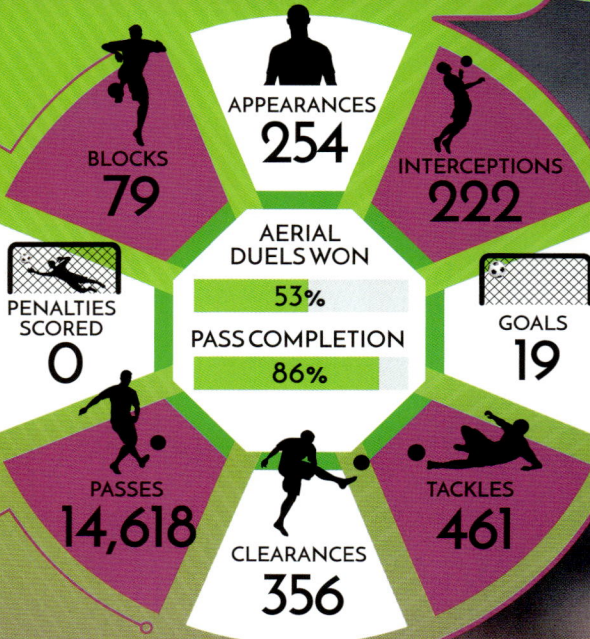

BLOCKS
79

APPEARANCES
254

INTERCEPTIONS
222

PENALTIES SCORED
0

AERIAL DUELS WON
53%

PASS COMPLETION
86%

GOALS
19

PASSES
14,618

CLEARANCES
356

TACKLES
461

MAJOR CLUB HONOURS
⚽ Serie A: 2023
⚽ Coppa Italia: 2020

INTERNATIONAL HONOURS
⚽ UEFA European Championship: 2020 (2021)
⚽ UEFA Nations League: third place 2021, 2023

ACTIVITY AREAS

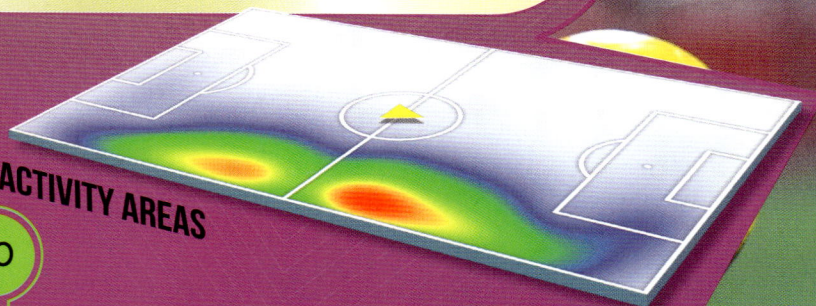

MARQUINHOS

Marquinhos is a clever defender. He may not be a powerhouse like many of today's top-class centre-backs but has the speed, agility and intelligence to mark the quickest forwards, plus he can be very effective going forward.

NATIONALITY
Brazilian

CURRENT CLUB
Paris Saint-Germain

5

DATE OF BIRTH	14/05/1994
POSITION	CENTRAL
HEIGHT	1.83 M
PRO DEBUT	2012
PREFERRED FOOT	RIGHT

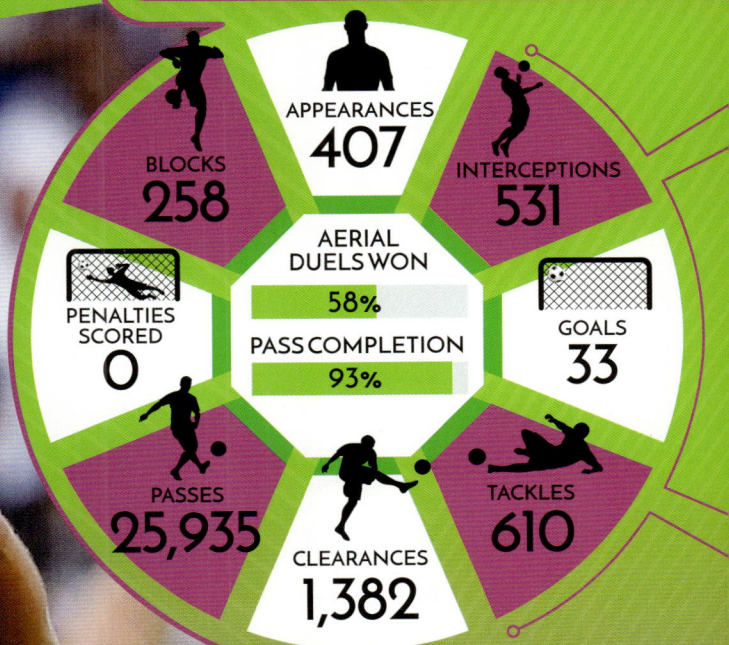

BLOCKS
258

APPEARANCES
407

INTERCEPTIONS
531

PENALTIES SCORED
0

AERIAL DUELS WON
58%

PASS COMPLETION
93%

GOALS
33

PASSES
25,935

CLEARANCES
1,382

TACKLES
610

MAJOR CLUB HONOURS
⚽ Ligue 1: 2014, 2015, 2016, 2018, 2019, 2020, 2022, 2023, 2024 ⚽ UEFA Champions League: runner-up 2020 ⚽ Coupe de France: 2015, 2016, 2017, 2018, runner-up 2019, 2020, 2021, 2024

INTERNATIONAL HONOURS
⚽ Copa América: 2019, runner-up 2021
⚽ Olympic Games: 2016

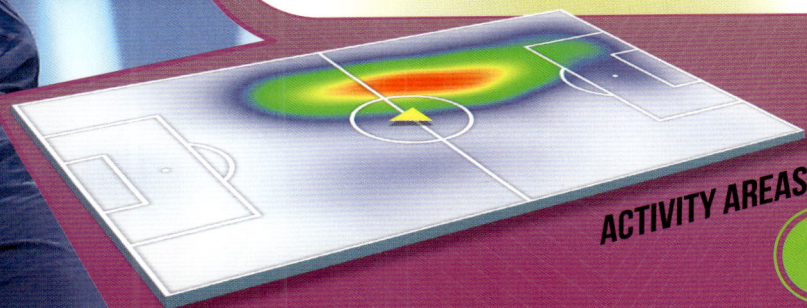

ACTIVITY AREAS

16

NATIONALITY
Argentinian

CURRENT CLUB
Atlético Madrid

NAHUEL MOLINA

Nahuel Molina has worked hard to become a dominant force on the right flank. Very quick, with fine positional sense and good tackling technique, he is also comfortable with the ball at his feet and a tremendous passer in attacking situations.

DATE OF BIRTH	06/04/1998
POSITION	RIGHT-BACK
HEIGHT	1.75 M
PRO DEBUT	2016
PREFERRED FOOT	RIGHT

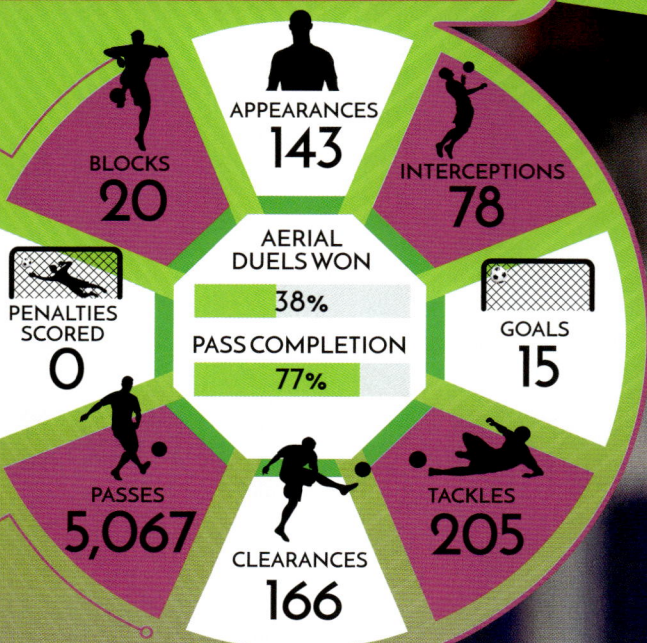

BLOCKS
20

APPEARANCES
143

INTERCEPTIONS
78

AERIAL DUELS WON
38%

PASS COMPLETION
77%

PENALTIES SCORED
0

GOALS
15

PASSES
5,067

CLEARANCES
166

TACKLES
205

MAJOR CLUB HONOURS
⚽ None to date

INTERNATIONAL HONOURS
⚽ FIFA World Cup: 2022
⚽ Copa América: 2021, 2024

ACTIVITY AREAS

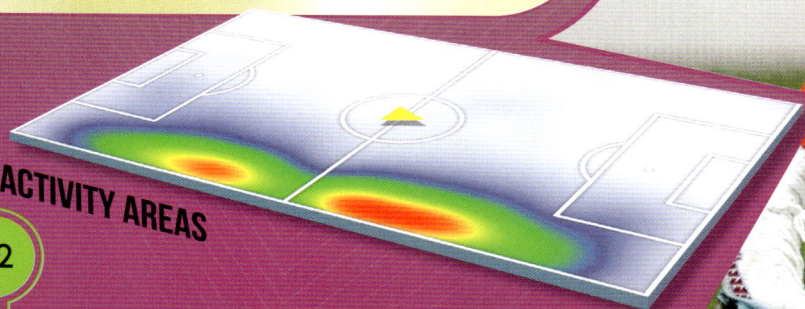

BENJAMIN PAVARD

Benjamin Pavard has matured into a technically brilliant defender. He has the ability to time his tackle perfectly and shut down opposing players in possession of the ball. He can also move the ball down one or two lines of defence with an incisive pass.

NATIONALITY
French

CURRENT CLUB
Inter Milan

28

DATE OF BIRTH	28/03/1996
PODITION	CENTRAL
HEIGHT	1.86 M
PRO DEBUT	2014
PREFERRED FOOT	RIGHT

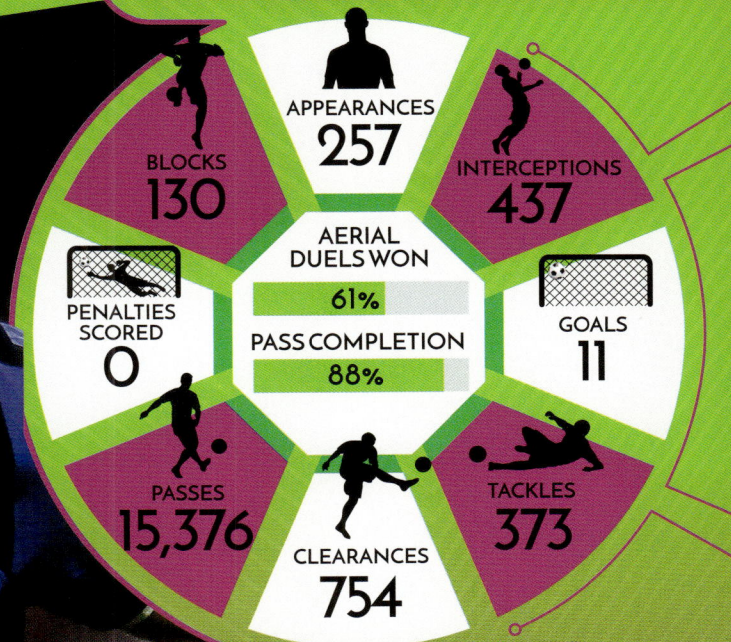

BLOCKS
130

APPEARANCES
257

INTERCEPTIONS
437

PENALTIES SCORED
0

AERIAL DUELS WON
61%

PASS COMPLETION
88%

GOALS
11

PASSES
15,376

CLEARANCES
754

TACKLES
373

MAJOR CLUB HONOURS
⚽ Serie A: 2024 ⚽ Bundesliga: 2020, 2021, 2022, 2023 (all B. Munich) ⚽ UEFA Champions League: 2020 (B. Munich) ⚽ UEFA Super Cup: 2020 (B. Munich) ⚽ FIFA Club World Cup: 2020 (B. Munich) ⚽ DFB-Pokal: 2020 (B. Munich)

INTERNATIONAL HONOURS
⚽ FIFA World Cup: 2018, runner-up 2022
⚽ UEFA Nations League: 2021

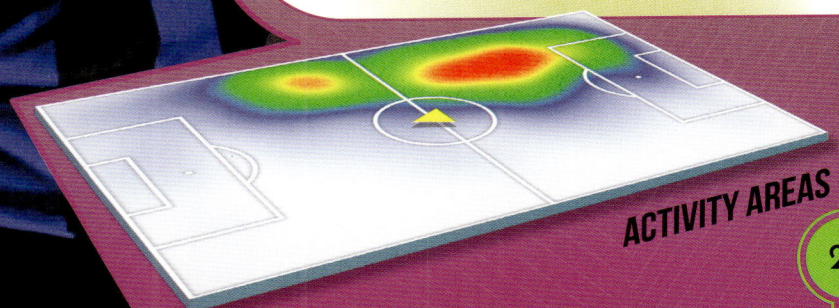

ACTIVITY AREAS

23

SERGIO RAMOS

NATIONALITY
Spanish

CURRENT CLUB
TBC

Very quick at anticipating danger, Sergio Ramos is a fine tackler with an excellent positional sense. Not only is he a skilled defender and great team leader, but is also known for regularly scoring important goals for his team. He left Sevilla after a season in 2024.

DATE OF BIRTH	30/03/1986
POSITION	CENTRAL
HEIGHT	1.84 M
PRO DEBUT	2003
PREFERRED FOOT	RIGHT

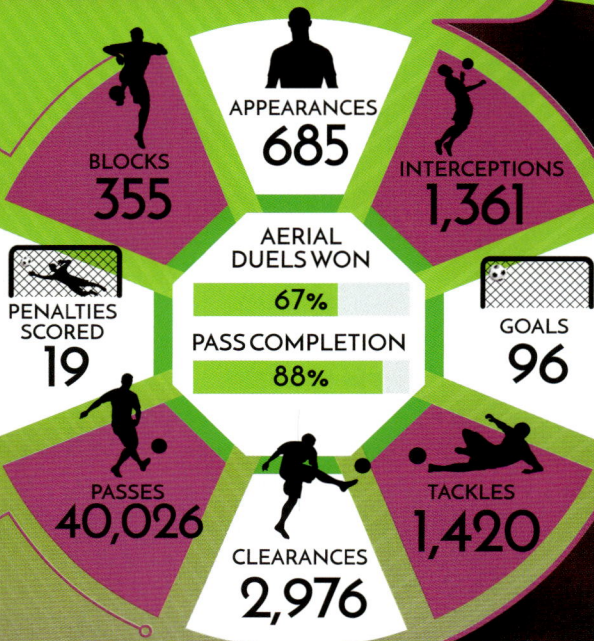

BLOCKS
355

APPEARANCES
685

INTERCEPTIONS
1,361

AERIAL DUELS WON
67%

PASS COMPLETION
88%

PENALTIES SCORED
19

GOALS
96

PASSES
40,026

CLEARANCES
2,976

TACKLES
1,420

MAJOR CLUB HONOURS

⚽ Ligue 1: 2022, 2023 (all PSG) ⚽ La Liga: 2007-08, 2012, 2017, 2020 (all R. Madrid) ⚽ UEFA Champions League: 2014, 2016, 2017, 2018 (all R. Madrid) ⚽ UEFA Super Cup: 2014, 2016, 2017 (all R. Madrid) ⚽ FIFA Club World Cup: 2014, 2016-18 (all R. Madrid)

INTERNATIONAL HONOURS

⚽ FIFA World Cup: 2010
⚽ UEFA European Championship: 2008, 2012
⚽ FIFA Confederations Cup: third place 2009, runner-up 2013

ACTIVITY AREAS

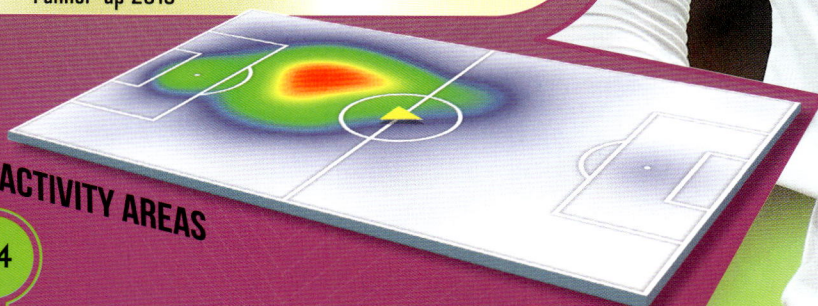

ANDREW ROBERTSON

NATIONALITY
Scottish

CURRENT CLUB
Liverpool

26

In a short space of time, Andrew Robertson has become one of the world's best left-sided defenders. He is fast and an excellent tackler and reader of the game, plus his ability to hare down the flank, complete neat one-twos and whip over dangerous crosses makes him an asset in attack.

DATE OF BIRTH	11/03/1994
POSITION	LEFT-BACK
HEIGHT	1.78 M
PRO DEBUT	2012
PREFERRED FOOT	LEFT

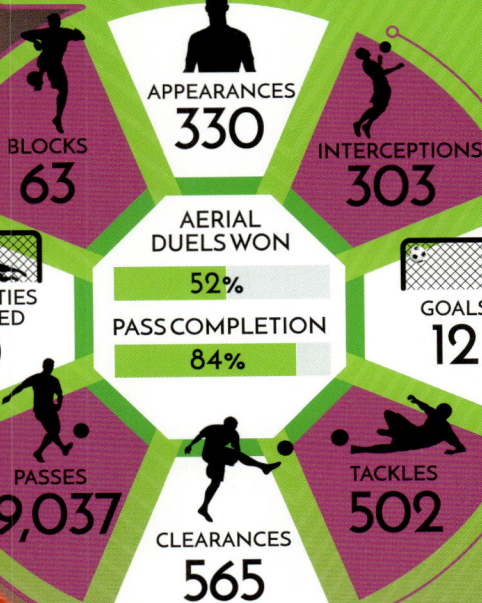

BLOCKS
63

APPEARANCES
330

INTERCEPTIONS
303

PENALTIES SCORED
0

AERIAL DUELS WON
52%

PASS COMPLETION
84%

GOALS
12

PASSES
19,037

CLEARANCES
565

TACKLES
502

MAJOR CLUB HONOURS
⚽ Premier League: 2020 ⚽ UEFA Champions League: 2019
⚽ FIFA World Club Cup: 2019 ⚽ UEFA Super Cup: 2019
⚽ FA Cup: 2022

INTERNATIONAL HONOURS
⚽ None to date

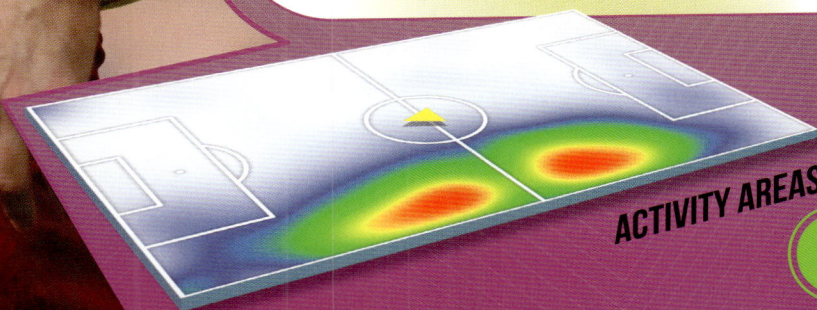

ACTIVITY AREAS

22

NATIONALITY
German

CURRENT CLUB
Real Madrid

ANTONIO RÜDIGER

Antonio Rüdiger has become a dominant defender all along the back line, winning tackles with his strength and dominating the penalty area with his heading ability. He is also an excellent passer, reads the game well and leads by example.

DATE OF BIRTH	03/03/1993
POSITION	CENTRAL
HEIGHT	1.90 M
PRO DEBUT	2011
PREFERRED FOOT	RIGHT

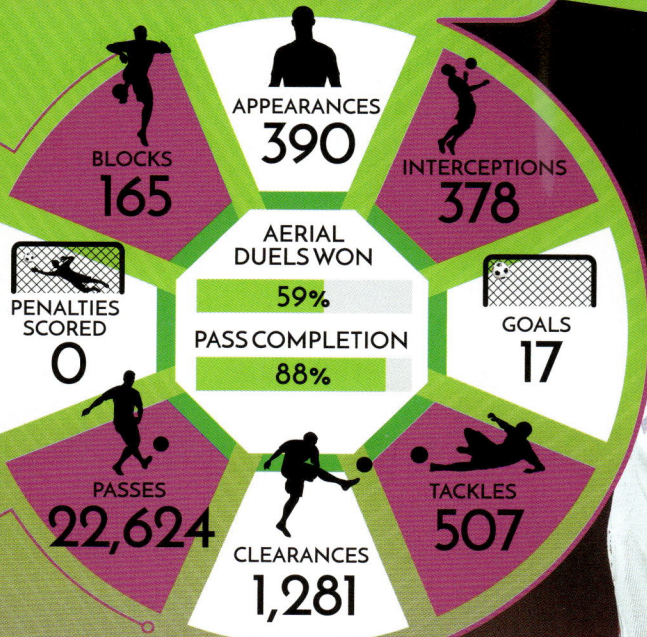

BLOCKS
165

APPEARANCES
390

INTERCEPTIONS
378

AERIAL DUELS WON
59%

PASS COMPLETION
88%

PENALTIES SCORED
0

GOALS
17

PASSES
22,624

CLEARANCES
1,281

TACKLES
507

MAJOR CLUB HONOURS

⚽ La Liga: 2024 ⚽ UEFA Champions League: 2021 (Chelsea), 2024 ⚽ FIFA World Club Cup: 2021 (Chelsea), 2022 ⚽ UEFA Europa League 2019 (Chelsea) ⚽ UEFA Super Cup: 2021 (Chelsea), 2022 ⚽ FA Cup: 2018 ⚽ Copa del Rey: 2023

INTERNATIONAL HONOURS

⚽ FIFA Confederations Cup: 2017

ACTIVITY AREAS

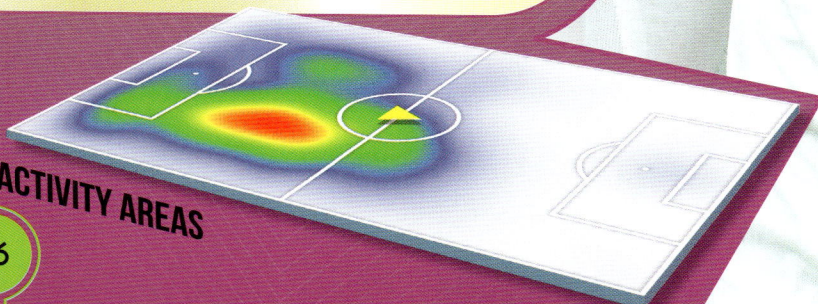

STEFAN SAVIĆ

Stefan Savić reads the game well but his biggest strength is his ability in the air. He is comfortable on the ball and neat with his short passing, relying on brains rather than brawn to operate effectively at the back.

NATIONALITY
Montenegran

CURRENT CLUB
Atlético Madrid

15

DATE OF BIRTH	08/01/1991
POSITION	CENTRAL
HEIGHT	1.87 M
PRO DEBUT	2009
PREFERRED FOOT	RIGHT

APPEARANCES
385

BLOCKS
221

INTERCEPTIONS
666

AERIAL DUELS WON
64%

PENALTIES SCORED
0

PASS COMPLETION
85%

GOALS
8

PASSES
17,003

CLEARANCES
1,789

TACKLES
504

MAJOR CLUB HONOURS
⚽ La Liga: 2021 ⚽ UEFA Champions League: runner-up 2016 ⚽ UEFA Europa League: 2018 ⚽ UEFA Super Cup: 2018 ⚽ Premier League: 2012 (Man City)

INTERNATIONAL HONOURS
⚽ None to date

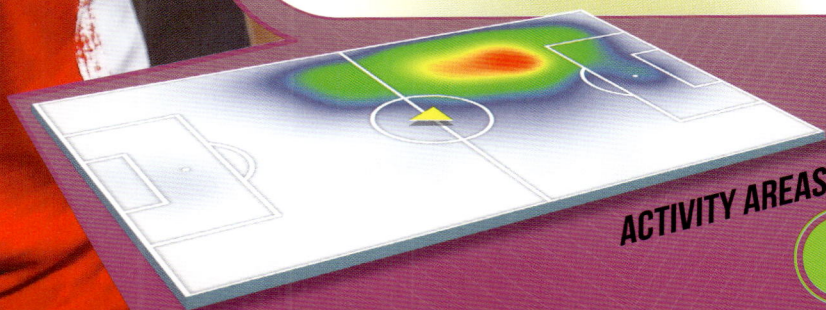

ACTIVITY AREAS

27

6

NATIONALITY
Brazilian

CURRENT CLUB
Fluminense

THIAGO SILVA

Players past and present rate Thiago Silva as one of the best-ever central defenders to play the game. In addition to his technical strengths, he is a natural leader who is able to inspire team-mates to raise their game in the heat of battle.

DATE OF BIRTH	22/09/1984
POSITION	CENTRAL
HEIGHT	1.83 M
PRO DEBUT	2002
PREFERRED FOOT	RIGHT

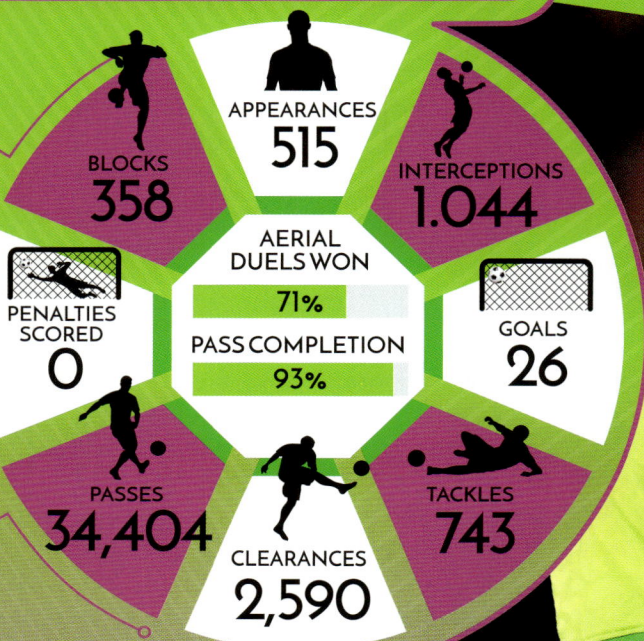

BLOCKS
358

APPEARANCES
515

INTERCEPTIONS
1,044

AERIAL DUELS WON
71%

PASS COMPLETION
93%

PENALTIES SCORED
0

GOALS
26

PASSES
34,404

TACKLES
743

CLEARANCES
2,590

MAJOR CLUB HONOURS
⚽ UEFA Champions League: 2021 (Chelsea), runner-up 2020 (PSG) ⚽ UEFA Super Cup: 2021 (Chelsea) ⚽ FIFA Club World Cup: 2021 (Chelsea) ⚽ Serie A: 2011 (AC Milan) ⚽ Ligue 1: 2013-2020 (PSG) ⚽ Coupe de France: 2015-18, 2020 (all PSG) ⚽ FA Cup: 2022 (Chelsea)

INTERNATIONAL HONOURS
⚽ FIFA Confederations Cup; 2013
⚽ Copa América: 2019, runner-up 2021

ACTIVITY AREAS

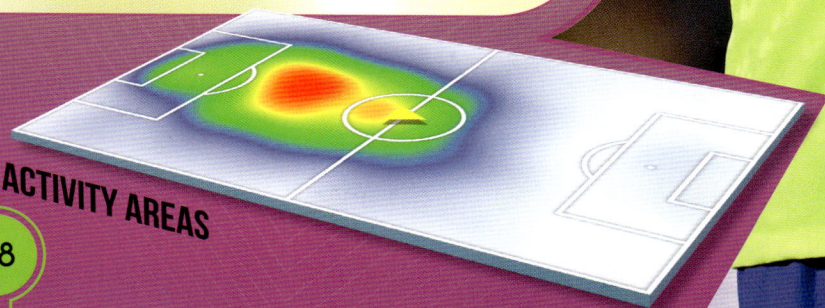

28

MILAN ŠKRINIAR

Centre-back Milan Škriniar is a forceful tackler, strong in the air and combative on the ground. But what sets Škriniar apart are his ball-playing skills, being able to stay calm under pressure and pick out intelligent passes.

NATIONALITY
Slovakian

CURRENT CLUB
Paris Saint-Germain

37

DATE OF BIRTH	11/02/1995
POSITION	CENTRAL
HEIGHT	1.87 M
PRO DEBUT	2012
PREFERRED FOOT	RIGHT

APPEARANCES
296

BLOCKS
194

INTERCEPTIONS
263

AERIAL DUELS WON
51%

PASS COMPLETION
92%

PENALTIES SCORED
0

GOALS
12

PASSES
18,455

CLEARANCES
947

TACKLES
466

MAJOR CLUB HONOURS

⚽ Ligue 1: 2024 ⚽ Serie A: 2021 (Inter Milan) ⚽ UEFA Champions League: runner-up 2023 (Inter Milan) ⚽ UEFA Europa League: runner-up 2020 (Inter Milan) ⚽ Coupe de France: 2024 ⚽ Coppa Italia: 2022, 2023 (Inter Milan)

INTERNATIONAL HONOURS

⚽ King's Cup: 2018

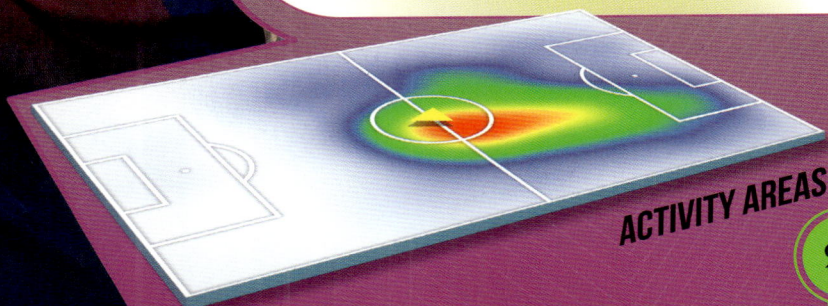

ACTIVITY AREAS

2

NATIONALITY
French

CURRENT CLUB
Bayern Munich

DAYOT UPAMECANO

Dayot Upamecano has developed into an exceptional centre-half with all the talents needed for the position. His standout talent is his ability with the ball at his feet — a quality that complements his passing accuracy.

DATE OF BIRTH	27/10/1998
POSITION	CENTRAL
HEIGHT	1.86 M
PRO DEBUT	2015
PREFERRED FOOT	RIGHT

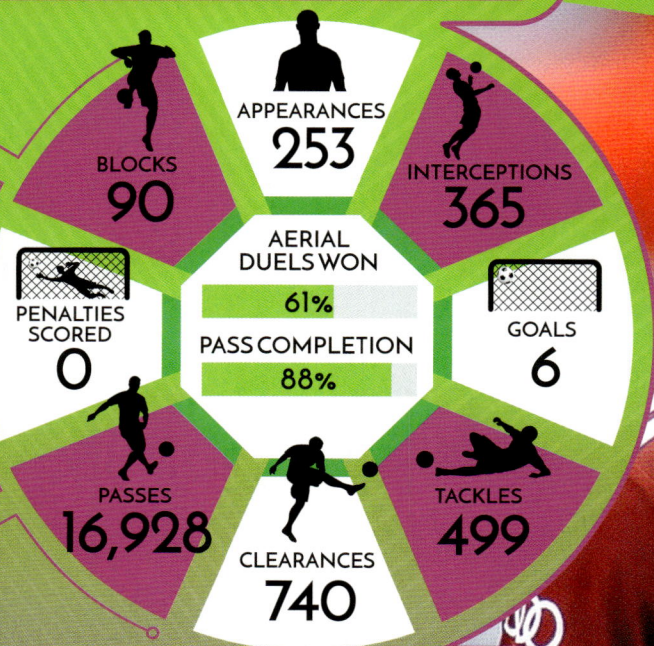

BLOCKS
90

APPEARANCES
253

INTERCEPTIONS
365

PENALTIES SCORED
0

AERIAL DUELS WON
61%

PASS COMPLETION
88%

GOALS
6

PASSES
16,928

CLEARANCES
740

TACKLES
499

MAJOR CLUB HONOURS
⚽ Bundesliga: 2022, 2023
⚽ DFL Supercup: 2021

INTERNATIONAL HONOURS
⚽ UEFA Nations League: 2021
⚽ FIFA World Cup: runner-up 2022

ACTIVITY AREAS

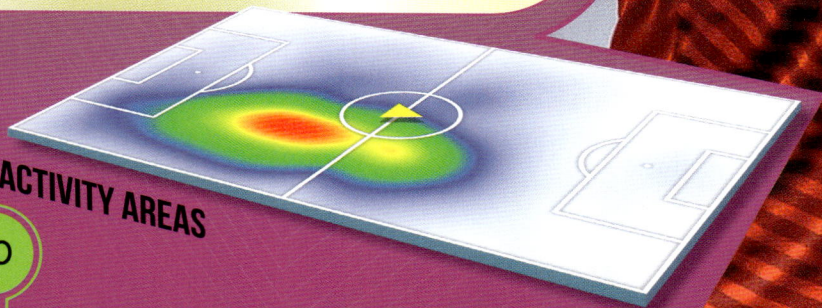

RAPHAËL VARANE

While most defenders peak in their late 20s, Raphaël Varane was already a star in his teens. Accurate with both feet, an excellent tackler and great in the air, Varane can also launch attacks with his sharp passing and even score goals. Varane left Manchester United in 2024 after three seasons.

NATIONALITY
French

CURRENT CLUB
TBC

DATE OF BIRTH	25/04/1993
POSITION	CENTRAL
HEIGHT	1.91 M
PRO DEBUT	2010
PREFERRED FOOT	RIGHT

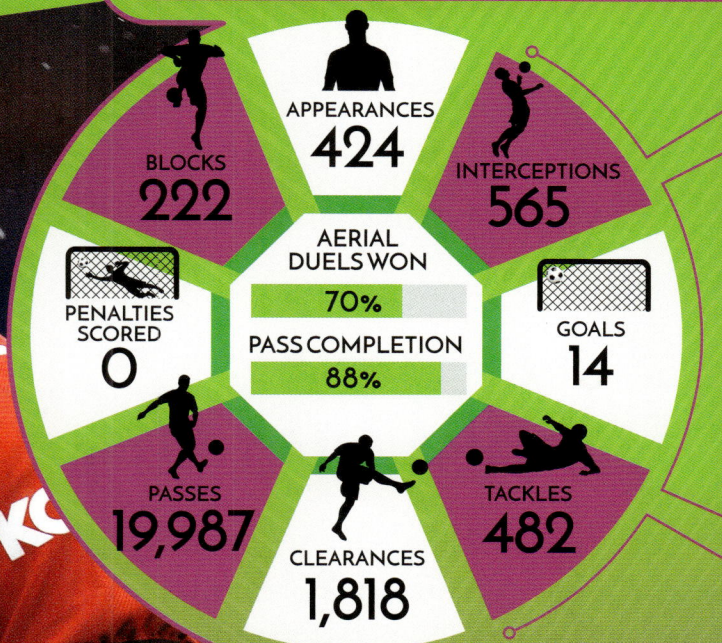

APPEARANCES
424

INTERCEPTIONS
565

BLOCKS
222

AERIAL DUELS WON
70%

PASS COMPLETION
88%

GOALS
14

PENALTIES SCORED
0

TACKLES
482

PASSES
19,987

CLEARANCES
1,818

MAJOR CLUB HONOURS
⚽ La Liga: 2012, 2017, 2020 (all R. Madrid) ⚽ UEFA Champions League: 2014, 2016, 2017, 2018 (all R. Madrid) ⚽ UEFA Super Cup: 2014, 2016, 2017 (all R. Madrid) ⚽ FIFA Club World Cup: 2014, 2016, 2017, 2018 (all R. Madrid) ⚽ FA Cup: runner-up 2023, 2024 (Man. Utd)

INTERNATIONAL HONOURS
⚽ FIFA World Cup: 2018, runner-up 2022
⚽ UEFA Nations League: 2021

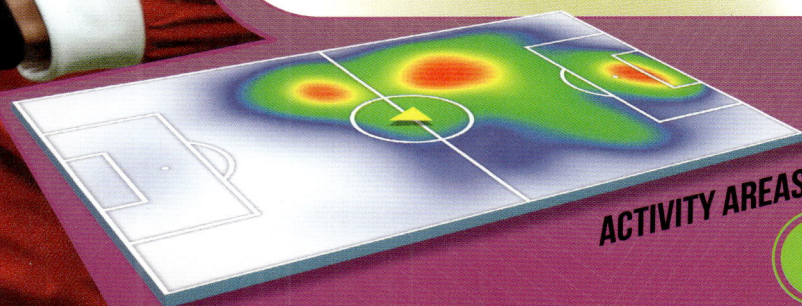

ACTIVITY AREAS

31

MIDFIELDERS

Midfielders are the heartbeat of a team. Not only do they play between the forwards and the defenders but they also help out their team-mates at both ends. Midfielders fall into one of four main categories: 1) defensive midfielders, who sit in front of the back four and are great tacklers; 2) the attacking full-backs operating on the wings, who whip crosses into the box; 3) the central midfielders, who are brilliant at setting up and then joining attacks, as well as helping out in defence whenever needed; 4) the playmakers — these are the stars who build the attack with their creative play.

WHAT DO THE STATS MEAN?

ASSISTS
A pass, cross or header to a team-mate who then scores counts as an assist. This stat also includes a deflected shot that is converted by a team-mate.

SHOTS
Any deliberate strike on goal counts as a shot. The strike does not have to be on target or force a save from the keeper.

CHANCES CREATED
Any pass that results in a shot at goal (whether or not the goal is scored) is regarded as a chance created.

TACKLES
This is the number of times the player has challenged and dispossessed the opposition without committing a foul.

DRIBBLES
This is the number of times the player has gone past an opponent while running with the ball.

SUCCESSFUL PASSES
75%
This shows as a percentage how successful the midfielder is at finding team-mates with passes, whether over 5 or 60 yards.

Did you know?

In top-level football, midfielders tend to cover the most ground during the course of a match. A midfielder playing the full 90 minutes will usually run anywhere between 9.5 and 12km.

5

NATIONALITY
English

CURRENT CLUB
Real Madrid

JUDE BELLINGHAM

Jude Bellingham's talent was evident when he was just 16 years old! Now he has fulfilled that promise and become one of the world's best midfielders playing for one of world's best clubs. He is a good tackler, exceptionally quick, positionally aware, and able to create and score goals.

DATE OF BIRTH	29/06/2003
POSITION	CENTRAL
HEIGHT	1.86 M
PRO DEBUT	2019
PREFERRED FOOT	RIGHT

ASSISTS
32

APPEARANCES
156

DRIBBLES
485

PENALTIES SCORED
2

PASSES
7247
SUCCESSFUL PASSES
85%

GOALS
43

SHOTS
271

CHANCES CREATED
184

TACKLES
296

MAJOR CLUB HONOURS
⚽ La Liga: 2024
⚽ UEFA Champions League: 2024
⚽ Bundesliga: runner-up 2023 (Borussia Dortmund)
⚽ DFB-Pokal: 2021 (Borussia Dortmund)

INTERNATIONAL HONOURS
⚽ UEFA European Championship: runner-up 2020 (2021), runner-up 2024

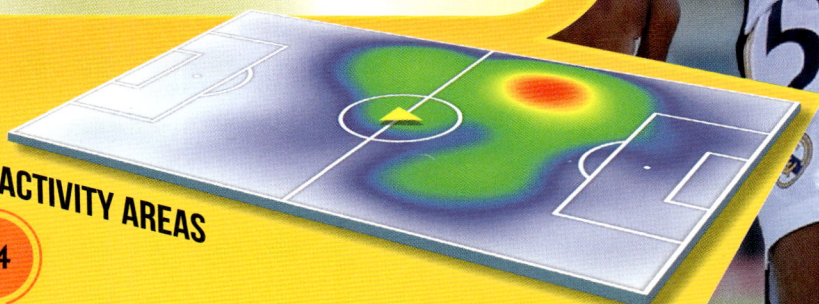

ACTIVITY AREAS

KEVIN DE BRUYNE

Kevin De Bruyne ranks as one of the finest attacking midfielders in the game today. Strong and technically brilliant, he can break up play at one end and almost immediately blast a 25-metre shot into the opposite goal. In 2024, he notched up his 100th goal for Manchester City.

NATIONALITY
Belgian

CURRENT CLUB
Manchester City

DATE OF BIRTH	28/06/1991
POSITION	ATTACKING
HEIGHT	1.81 M
PRO DEBUT	2008
PREFERRED FOOT	RIGHT

APPEARANCES
428

ASSISTS
177

DRIBBLES
1,249

PASSES
20,607

SUCCESSFUL PASSES
81%

PENALTIES SCORED
5

GOALS
112

SHOTS
1,035

CHANCES CREATED
1,246

TACKLES
508

MAJOR CLUB HONOURS
- ⚽ Premier League: 2018, 2019, 2021, 2022, 2023, 2024
- ⚽ UEFA Champions League: runner-up 2021, 2023
- ⚽ FA Cup: 2019, 2023

INTERNATIONAL HONOURS
- ⚽ FIFA World Cup: third place 2018

ACTIVITY AREAS

5

NATIONALITY
Spanish

CURRENT CLUB
Inter Miami

SERGIO BUSQUETS

Sergio Busquets plays as a deep midfielder who dictates the team's build-up play with clever, short and longer passes. He is great at stopping attacks before they become dangerous and then making passes to launch his team's raids.

DATE OF BIRTH	16/07/1988
POSITION	DEFENSIVE
HEIGHT	1.89 M
PRO DEBUT	2007
PREFERRED FOOT	RIGHT

APPEARANCES
645

ASSISTS
45

DRIBBLES
441

PASSES
46,099
SUCCESSFUL PASSES
91%

PENALTIES SCORED
0

GOALS
17

SHOTS
155

CHANCES CREATED
417

TACKLES
1,650

MAJOR CLUB HONOURS

⚽ La Liga: 2009-11, 2013, 2015 2016, 2018, 2019, 2023 (All Barça)
⚽ UEFA Champions League: 2009, 2011, 2015 (all Barça) ⚽ UEFA Super Cup: 2009, 2011, 2015 (all Barça) ⚽ FIFA Club World Cup: 2009, 2011, 2015 (all Barça) ⚽ MLS Leagues Cup: 2023

INTERNATIONAL HONOURS

⚽ FIFA World Cup: 2010 ⚽ UEFA European Championship: 2012 ⚽ FIFA Confederations Cup: runner up 2013 ⚽ UEFA Nations League: runner-up 2021

ACTIVITY AREAS

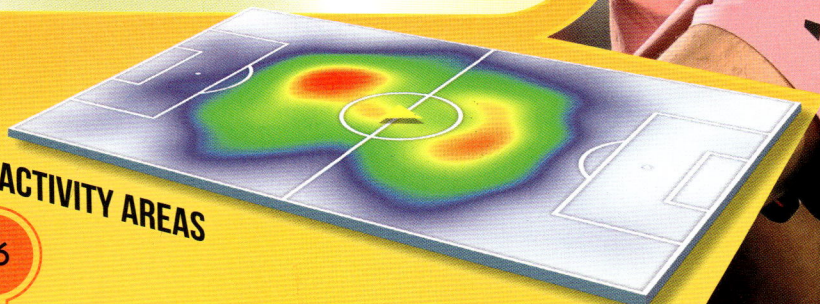

EMRE CAN

Having been a defender earlier in his career, Emre Can has grown into a classy central midfielder. He combines his excellent tackling strength with his midfielder's instincts to thread passes to team-mates in attacking positions.

NATIONALITY
German

CURRENT CLUB
Borussia Dortmund

23

DATE OF BIRTH	12/01/1994
POSITION	CENTRAL
HEIGHT	1.86 M
PRO DEBUT	2011
PREFERRED FOOT	RIGHT

APPEARANCES
369

ASSISTS
20

DRIBBLES
615

PASSES
18,346
SUCCESSFUL PASSES
85%

PENALTIES SCORED
8

GOALS
32

SHOTS
327

CHANCES CREATED
235

TACKLES
802

MAJOR CLUB HONOURS

⚽ Bundesliga: 2013 (B. Munich), runner-up 2023 ⚽ UEFA Champions League: 2013 (B. Munich), runner-up 2018 (Liverpool), runner-up 2024 ⚽ UEFA Europa League: runner-up 2016 (Liverpool) ⚽ Serie A: 2019, 2020 (Juventus) ⚽ DFB-Pokal: 2013 (B. Munich) 2021

INTERNATIONAL HONOURS

⚽ FIFA Confederations Cup: 2017

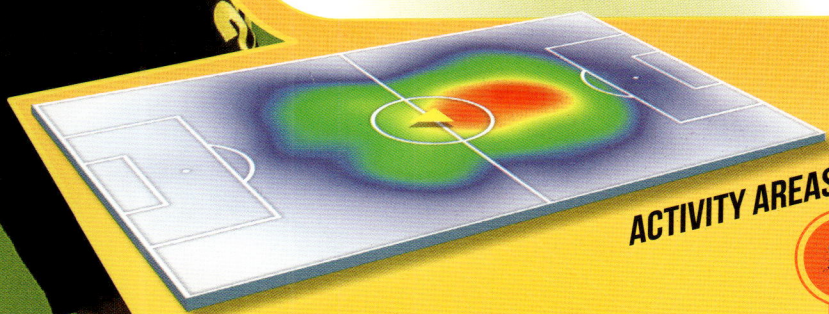

ACTIVITY AREAS

18

NATIONALITY
Brazilian

CURRENT CLUB
Manchester United

CASEMIRO

Casemiro's strengths are his great energy, high work rate and good support play. Strong, mobile and hard-tackling, his best position is as a defensive midfielder, though his mobility helps him get from box to box and he can also play at centre-back.

DATE OF BIRTH	23/02/1992
POSITION	CENTRAL
HEIGHT	1.85 M
PRO DEBUT	2010
PREFERRED FOOT	RIGHT

ASSISTS
28

APPEARANCES
370

DRIBBLES
271

PENALTIES SCORED
0

PASSES
19,756
SUCCESSFUL PASSES
85%

GOALS
38

SHOTS
429

CHANCES CREATED
236

TACKLES
1,127

MAJOR CLUB HONOURS
⚽ La Liga: 2017, 2020, 2022 (all R. Madrid) ⚽ UEFA Champs League: 2014, 2016, 2017, 2018, 2022 (all R. Madrid) ⚽ UEFA Super Cup: 2016, 2017, 2022 (all R. Madrid) ⚽ FIFA Club World Cup: 2016, 2017, 2018 (all R. Madrid) ⚽ FA Cup: runner-up 2023, 2024

INTERNATIONAL HONOURS
⚽ FIFA U-20 World Cup: 2011
⚽ Copa América: 2019, runner-up 2021

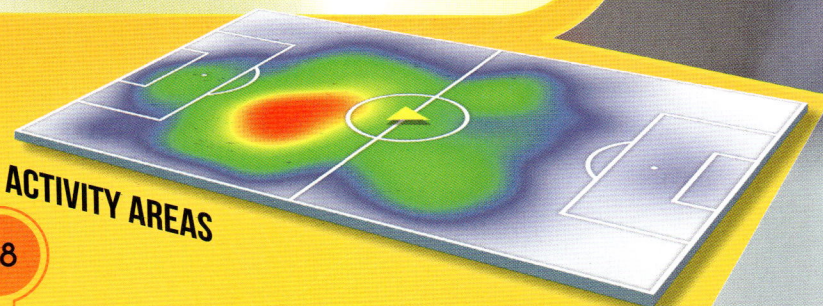

ACTIVITY AREAS

ALPHONSO DAVIES

Ghana-born Alphonso Davies is already considered one of the finest male footballers to represent Canada. He is equally productive and confident at all left-sided positions thanks to his great pace, dribbling talent, passing creativity, stamina and crossing ability.

NATIONALITY
Canadian

CURRENT CLUB
Bayern Munich

19

DATE OF BIRTH	02/11/2000
POSITION	LEFT WING
HEIGHT	1.83 M
PRO DEBUT	2016
PREFERRED FOOT	LEFT

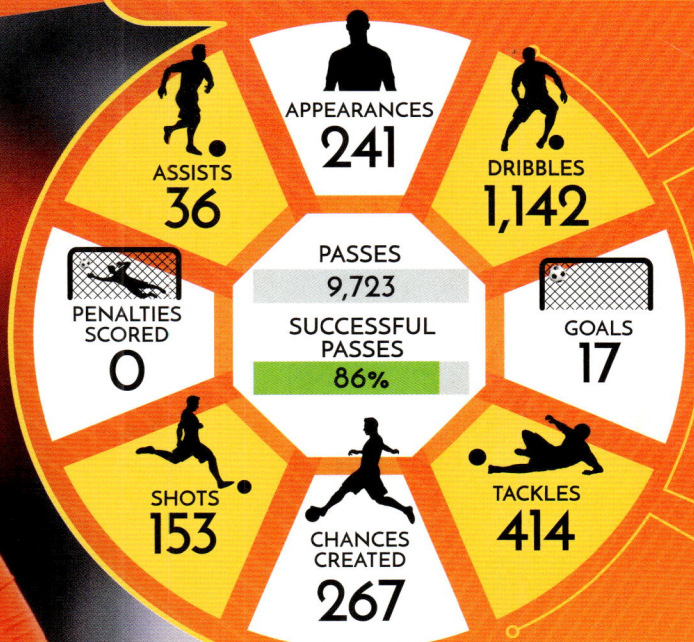

APPEARANCES
241

ASSISTS
36

DRIBBLES
1,142

PENALTIES SCORED
0

PASSES
9,723
SUCCESSFUL PASSES
86%

GOALS
17

SHOTS
153

CHANCES CREATED
267

TACKLES
414

MAJOR CLUB HONOURS

⚽ Bundesliga: 2019, 2020, 2021, 2022, 2023 ⚽ UEFA Champions League: 2020 ⚽ FIFA Club World Cup 2020 ⚽ UEFA Super Cup: 2020 ⚽ DFB-Pokal: 2019, 2020

INTERNATIONAL HONOURS

⚽ None to date

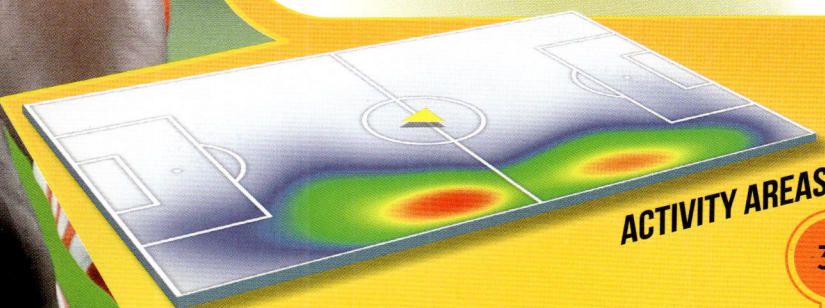

ACTIVITY AREAS

NATIONALITY
French

CURRENT CLUB
Paris Saint-Germain

OUSMANE DEMBÉLÉ

Ousmane Dembélé's speed, dribbling skills and ability to take on defenders make him a natural winger. Capable of playing on either flank, he frequently uses his pace and technical skills to create goal-scoring opportunities for himself or provide key passes and assists to his team-mates.

DATE OF BIRTH	15/05/1997
POSITION	WINGER
HEIGHT	1.78 M
PRO DEBUT	2014
PREFERRED FOOT	BOTH

APPEARANCES
268

ASSISTS
71

DRIBBLES
1,348

PASSES
7,936
SUCCESSFUL PASSES
80%

PENALTIES SCORED
2

GOALS
57

SHOTS
489

CHANCES CREATED
464

TACKLES
208

MAJOR CLUB HONOURS

⚽ Ligue 1: 2024 ⚽ La Liga: 2018, 2019, 2023 (all Barcelona) ⚽ Coupe de France: 2024 ⚽ Copa del Rey: 2018, 2021 (all Barcelona) ⚽ DFB Pokal: 2017 (Borussia Dortmund)

INTERNATIONAL HONOURS

⚽ FIFA World Cup: 2018, runner-up 2022

ACTIVITY AREAS

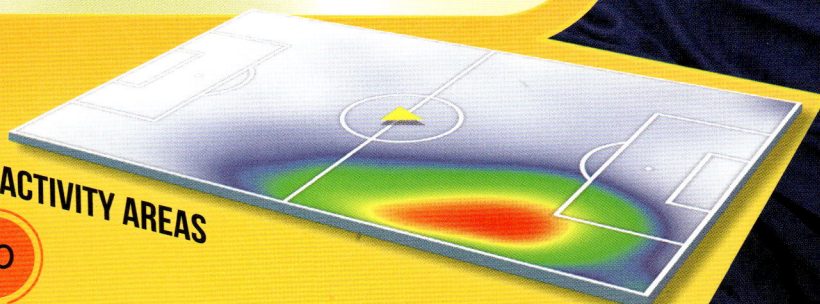

BRUNO FERNANDES

Bruno Fernandes shines as a central or attacking midfielder. A sound defensive player, he has a fantastic eye for creating chances with through balls, driving powerful shots from long range and is superb with penalties and free-kicks.

NATIONALITY
Portuguese

CURRENT CLUB
Manchester United

8

DATE OF BIRTH	08/09/1994
POSITION	ATTACKING
HEIGHT	1.79 M
PRO DEBUT	2012
PREFERRED FOOT	RIGHT

APPEARANCES
347*

ASSISTS
79

DRIBBLES
595

PENALTIES SCORED
31

PASSES
15,146
SUCCESSFUL PASSES
77%

GOALS
96

SHOTS
852

CHANCES CREATED
775

TACKLES
534

*Excludes data from Portuguese Premeira League

MAJOR CLUB HONOURS
⚽ UEFA Europa League: runner-up 2021 ⚽ Taça de Portugal: 2019 (Sporting CP) ⚽ Taça de Liga: 2018, 2019 (Sporting CP) ⚽ FA Cup: runner-up 2023, 2024

INTERNATIONAL HONOURS
⚽ UEFA Nations League: 2019

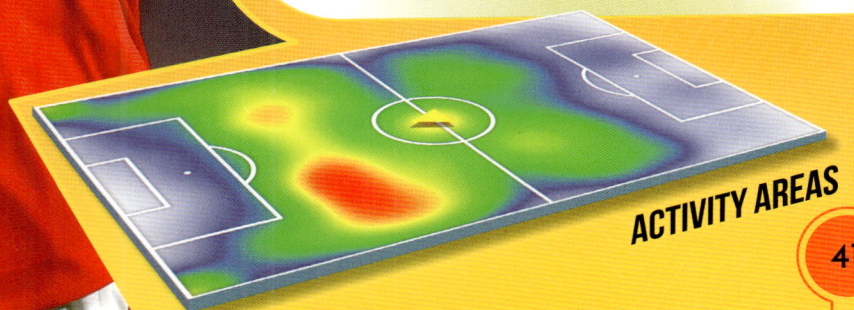

ACTIVITY AREAS

41

8

NATIONALITY
Argentinian

CURRENT CLUB
Chelsea

ENZO FERNÁNDEZ

Enzo Fernandez has enjoyed a meteoric rise, highlighted by his award as FIFA Best Young Player at the 2022 World Cup. Playing in central midfield, he is happy to help his defenders, while his exceptionally accurate long-range passing often launches dangerous attacks.

DATE OF BIRTH	17/01/2001
POSITION	CENTRAL
HEIGHT	1.78 M
PRO DEBUT	2019
PREFERRED FOOT	RIGHT

ASSISTS
5

APPEARANCES
55*

DRIBBLES
87

PASSES
3,804
SUCCESSFUL PASSES
88%

PENALTIES SCORED
1

GOALS
3

SHOTS
86

CHANCES CREATED
58

TACKLES
122

*Excludes data from Argentine and Portuguese Leagues

MAJOR CLUB HONOURS
⚽ Argentina Primera División: 2021 (River Plate)

INTERNATIONAL HONOURS
⚽ FIFA World Cup: 2022
⚽ Copa América: 2024

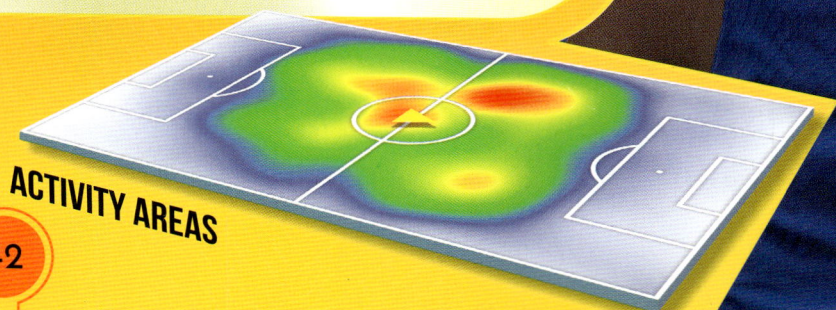

ACTIVITY AREAS

YOUSSOUF FOFANA

A commanding presence in the middle of the park, Youssouf Fofana plays a key role for both club and country. He is known for his box-to-box presence and is comfortable taking a leadership role, orchestrating the play and controlling the tempo of the match.

NATIONALITY
French

CURRENT CLUB
Monaco

19

DATE OF BIRTH	10/01/1999
POSITION	CENTRAL
HEIGHT	1.85 M
PRO DEBUT	2017
PREFERRED FOOT	RIGHT

APPEARANCES
186

ASSISTS
16

DRIBBLES
380

PASSES
7,941

SUCCESSFUL PASSES
82%

PENALTIES SCORED
0

GOALS
10

SHOTS
211

CHANCES CREATED
148

TACKLES
394

MAJOR CLUB HONOURS
⚽ Coupe De La Ligue: 2019

INTERNATIONAL HONOURS
⚽ FIFA World Cup: runner-up 2022

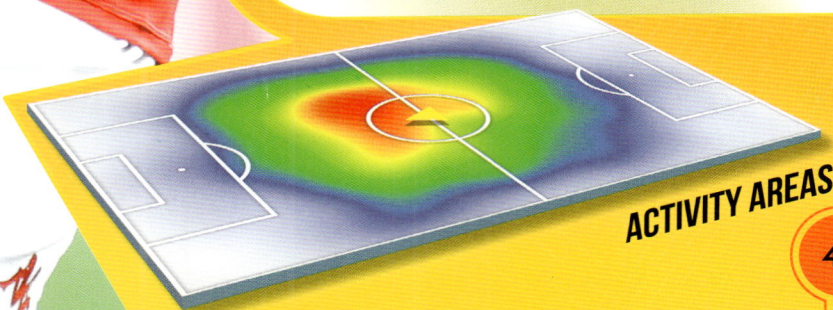

ACTIVITY AREAS

43

10

JACK GREALISH

Jack Grealish is among the finest attacking midfielders in Europe. He displays tight ball control, dribbling ability, change of speed and can shoot or deliver dangerous balls into the penalty area from the right or central positions.

DATE OF BIRTH	10/09/1995
POSITION	ATTACKING
HEIGHT	1.75 M
PRO DEBUT	2013
PREFERRED FOOT	RIGHT

ASSISTS
32

APPEARANCES
198

DRIBBLES
576

PENALTIES SCORED
0

PASSES
6,501
SUCCESSFUL PASSES
87%

GOALS
27

SHOTS
299

CHANCES CREATED
395

TACKLES
152

MAJOR CLUB HONOURS
⚽ Premier League: 2022, 2023, 2024 ⚽ UEFA Champions League: 2023 ⚽ FA Cup: runner-up 2015 (Aston Villa), 2023, runner-up 2024

INTERNATIONAL HONOURS
⚽ UEFA European Championship: runner-up 2020 (2021)

ACTIVITY AREAS

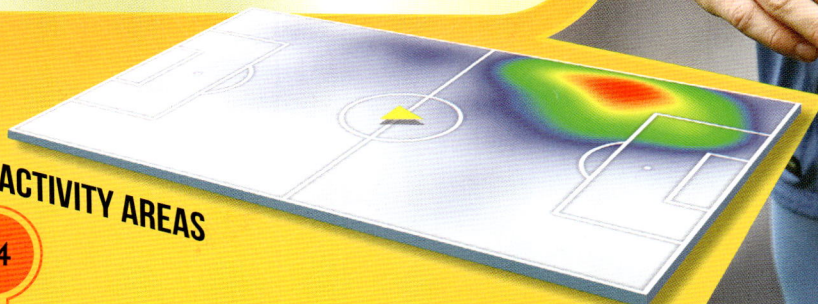

İLKAY GÜNDOĞAN

Although İlkay Gündoğan became a superstar quite late in his career, his team-mates have always recognised his value. Admired for his solid defensive talent, great energy, passing ability and reading situations, he has also developed a knack for scoring vital goals.

NATIONALITY
German

CURRENT CLUB
Barcelona

22

DATE OF BIRTH	24/10/1990
POSITION	CENTRAL
HEIGHT	1.80 M
PRO DEBUT	2008
PREFERRED FOOT	RIGHT

APPEARANCES
479

ASSISTS
56

DRIBBLES
881

PASSES
26,868

PENALTIES SCORED
5

SUCCESSFUL PASSES
89%

GOALS
76

SHOTS
692

CHANCES CREATED
611

TACKLES
617

MAJOR CLUB HONOURS
⚽ UEFA Champions League: 2023 (Man. City), runner-up 2021 (Man. City), runner-up 2013 (B. Dortmund) ⚽ Premier League: 2018, 2019, 2021-23 (all Man. City) ⚽ Bundesliga: 2012 (B. Dortmund)
⚽ FA Cup: 2018, 2019 (Man City) ⚽ DFB-Pokal: 2012 (B. Dortmund)

INTERNATIONAL HONOURS
⚽ None to date

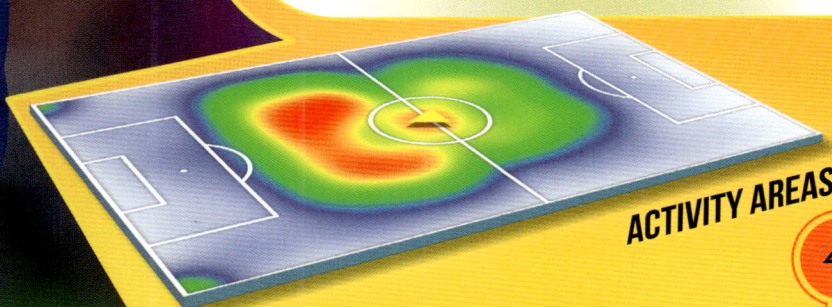

ACTIVITY AREAS

NATIONALITY
Dutch

CURRENT CLUB
Barcelona

FRENKIE DE JONG

Frenkie de Jong has been an outstanding talent ever since he burst on to the scene as a teenager. His close control, work rate, passing accuracy and movement have seen him being compared to the great Johan Cruyff.

DATE OF BIRTH	12/05/1997
POSITION	CENTRAL
HEIGHT	1.80 M
PRO DEBUT	2015
PREFERRED FOOT	RIGHT

ASSISTS
26

APPEARANCES
264

DRIBBLES
509

PENALTIES SCORED
0

PASSES
17,007

SUCCESSFUL PASSES
92%

GOALS
17

SHOTS
126

CHANCES CREATED
309

TACKLES
375

MAJOR CLUB HONOURS

⚽ La Liga: 2023 ✪ UEFA Europa League: runner-up 2017 (Ajax) ✪ Copa del Rey: 2021 ⚽ Eredivisie: 2019 (Ajax) ⚽ KNVB Cup: 2019 (Ajax)

INTERNATIONAL HONOURS

✪ UEFA Nations League: runner-up: 2019

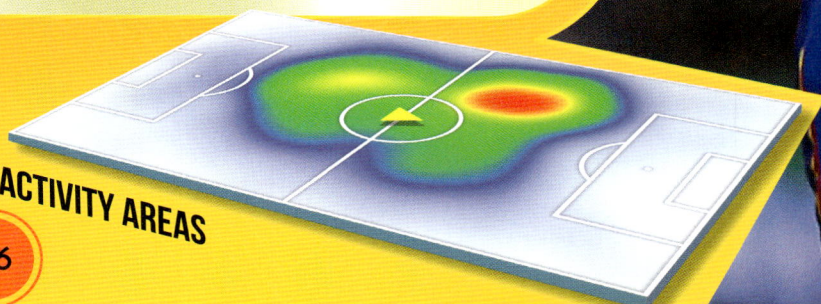

ACTIVITY AREAS

JORGINHO

The talented Jorginho can control the tempo of play from deep, link defence with midfield and midfield with attack with his accurate passing. He has the awareness, vision and passing ability to break lines, and can deliver lofted balls to attacking team-mates.

NATIONALITY
Italian

CURRENT CLUB
Arsenal

20

DATE OF BIRTH	20/12/1991
POSITION	DEFENSIVE
HEIGHT	1.80 M
PRO DEBUT	2010
PREFERRED FOOT	BOTH

APPEARANCES
402

ASSISTS
28

DRIBBLES
291

PENALTIES SCORED
33

PASSES
28,305
SUCCESSFUL PASSES
89%

GOALS
38

SHOTS
173

CHANCES CREATED
394

TACKLES
799

MAJOR CLUB HONOURS

⚽ Premier League: runner-up 2023, runner-up 2024 ⚽ UEFA Champs League: 2021 (Chelsea) ⚽ UEFA Europa League: 2019 (Chelsea) ⚽ FIFA World Club Cup: 2021 (Chelsea) ⚽ UEFA Super Cup: 2021 (Chelsea) ⚽ FA Cup: runner-up 2020-22 (Chelsea) ⚽ Coppa Italia: 2014 (Napoli)

INTERNATIONAL HONOURS

⚽ UEFA European Championship: 2020
⚽ UEFA Nations League: third place 2021, third place 2023

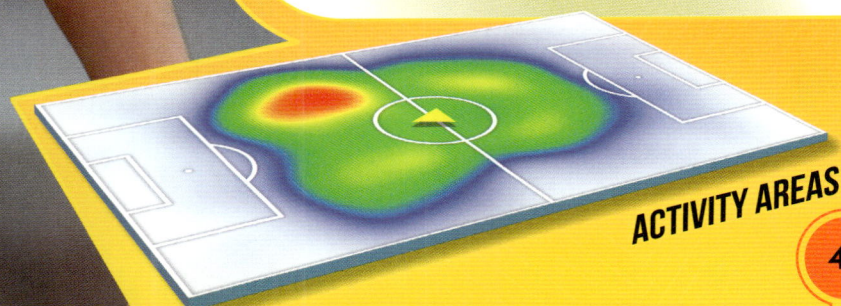

ACTIVITY AREAS

47

TONI KROOS

A set piece specialist who wins challenges in both boxes and dictates the game, Toni Kroos is an athletic box-to-box midfielder who can can pass long and short with either foot. He possesses great vision, creativity and energy.

DATE OF BIRTH	04/01/1990
POSITION	CENTRAL
HEIGHT	1.83 M
PRO DEBUT	2007
PREFERRED FOOT	RIGHT

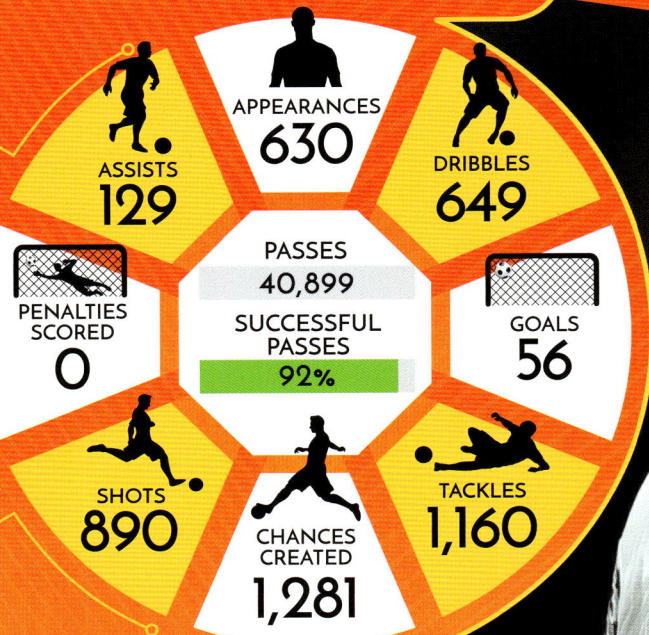

ASSISTS
129

APPEARANCES
630

DRIBBLES
649

PENALTIES SCORED
0

PASSES
40,899
SUCCESSFUL PASSES
92%

GOALS
56

SHOTS
890

CHANCES CREATED
1,281

TACKLES
1,160

MAJOR CLUB HONOURS
⚽ La Liga: 2017, 2020, 2022, 2024 (all R. Madrid) ⚽ Bundesliga: 2008, 2013, '14 (all B. Munich) ⚽ UEFA Champs League.: 2013 (B. Munich), 2016, '17, '18, '22, '24 (all R.Madrid) ⚽ FIFA Club WC: 2013 (B. Munich), 2014, '16, '17 '18, 2022 ⚽ UEFA Super Cup: 2013 (B. Mun), 2014, '17, '22 (all R. Mad.)

INTERNATIONAL HONOURS
⚽ FIFA World Cup: 2014

ACTIVITY AREAS

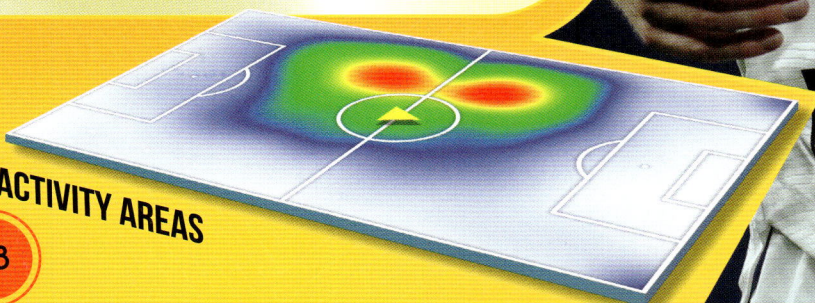

LUKA MODRIĆ

A top player for more than 20 years and a former Ballon d'Or winner (2018), Luka Modrić is still capable of determining the outcome of a match. He has a great footballing brain, can deliver long and short passes with both feet and strike powerful long-range shots, especially free-kicks.

NATIONALITY
Croatian

CURRENT CLUB
Real Madrid

10

DATE OF BIRTH	09/09/1985
POSITION	ATTACKING
HEIGHT	1.72 M
PRO DEBUT	2003
PREFERRED FOOT	RIGHT

APPEARANCES
616

ASSISTS
90

DRIBBLES
1,451

PASSES
34,352

SUCCESSFUL PASSES
89%

PENALTIES SCORED
5

GOALS
51

SHOTS
728

CHANCES CREATED
964

TACKLES
790

MAJOR CLUB HONOURS
⚽ La Liga: 2017, 2020, 2022, runner-up 2023, 2024 ⚽ UEFA Champions League: 2014, 2016, 2017, 2018, 2022, 2024 ⚽ UEFA Super Cup: 2014, 2016, 2017, 2022 ⚽ FIFA Club World Cup: 2014, 2016, 2017, 2018, 2022 ⚽ Copa del Rey: 2023

INTERNATIONAL HONOURS
⚽ FIFA World Cup: runner-up 2018, third place 2022
⚽ UEFA Nations League: runner-up 2023

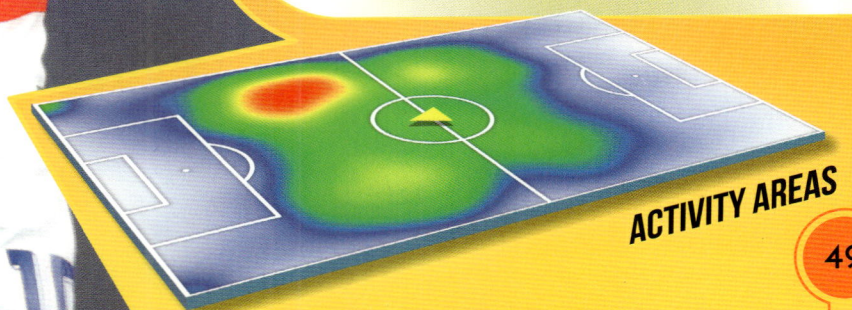

ACTIVITY AREAS

25

NATIONALITY
German

CURRENT CLUB
Bayern Munich

THOMAS MÜLLER

Thomas Müller is a dangerous attacking midfielder, who scores countless goals playing just behind a lone striker. The German powerhouse is mentally strong, tactically clever and great at finding holes in the opposition's defence.

DATE OF BIRTH	13/09/1989
POSITION	SECOND STRIKER
HEIGHT	1.85 M
PRO DEBUT	2008
PREFERRED FOOT	RIGHT

ASSISTS
193

APPEARANCES
624

DRIBBLES
1,046

PENALTIES SCORED
22

PASSES
20,004
SUCCESSFUL PASSES
77%

GOALS
203

SHOTS
1,196

CHANCES CREATED
1,168

TACKLES
645

MAJOR CLUB HONOURS

⚽ Bundesliga: 2010, 2013, 2014, 2015, 2016, 2017, 2018, 2019, 2020, 2021, 2022, 2023 ⚽ DFB-Pokal: 2010, 2013, 2014, 2016, 2019, 2020 ⚽ UEFA Champions League: runner-up 2010, runner-up 2012, 2013, 2020 ⚽ FIFA Club World Cup: 2013, 2020

INTERNATIONAL HONOURS

⚽ FIFA World Cup: 2014, third place 2010

ACTIVITY AREAS

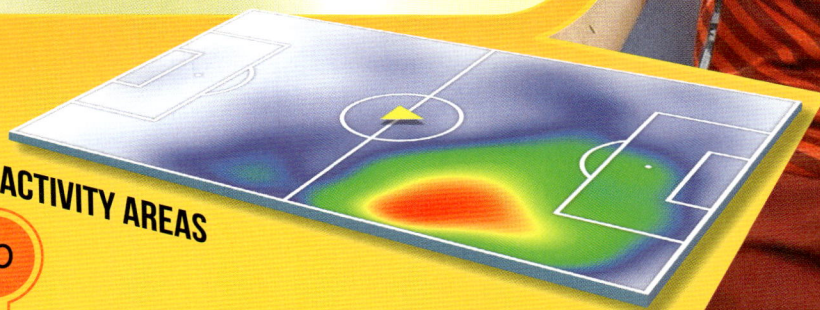

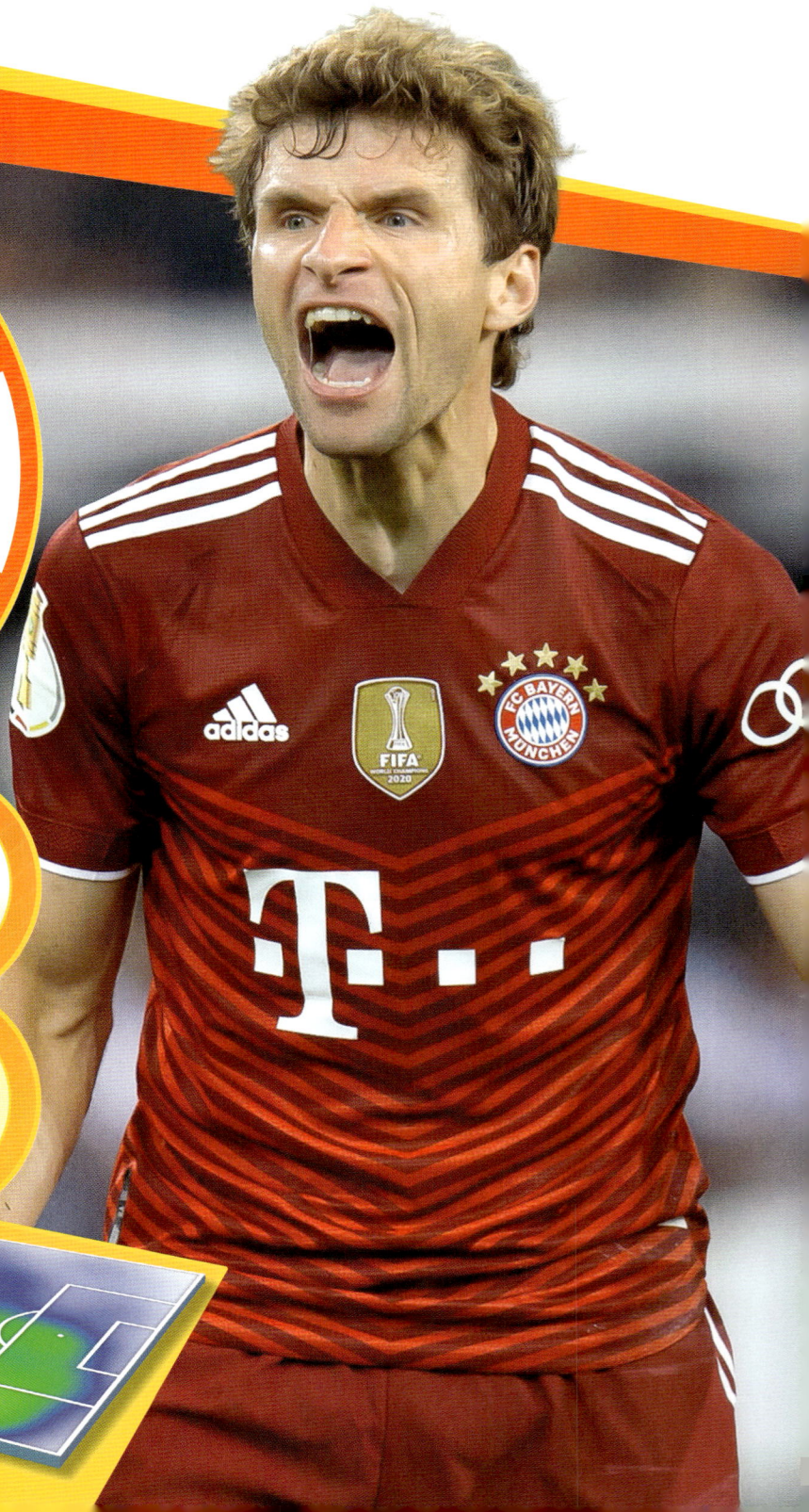

CHRISTIAN PULISIC

Although capable of playing in any attacking position, Christian Pulisic's pace, agility and technical ability have made him most effective on the left wing. He also likes to have the ball at his feet, dribbling past opponents to create shooting opportunities for himself.

NATIONALITY
American

CURRENT CLUB
AC Milan

11

DATE OF BIRTH	18/09/1998
POSITION	RIGHT
HEIGHT	1.79 M
PRO DEBUT	2016
PREFERRED FOOT	BOTH

ASSISTS
41

APPEARANCES
290

DRIBBLES
1,142

PENALTIES SCORED
0

PASSES
6,439
SUCCESSFUL PASSES
80%

GOALS
55

SHOTS
409

CHANCES CREATED
277

TACKLES
256

MAJOR CLUB HONOURS
⚽ UEFA Champions League: 2021 (Chelsea) ⚽ UEFA Super Cup: 2021 (Chelsea) ⚽ FIFA Club World Cup: 2021 (Chelsea) ⚽ DFB-Pokal: 2017 (Borussia Dortmund)

INTERNATIONAL HONOURS
⚽ CONCACAF Nations League: 2020
⚽ ONCACAF Gold Cup: runner-up 2019

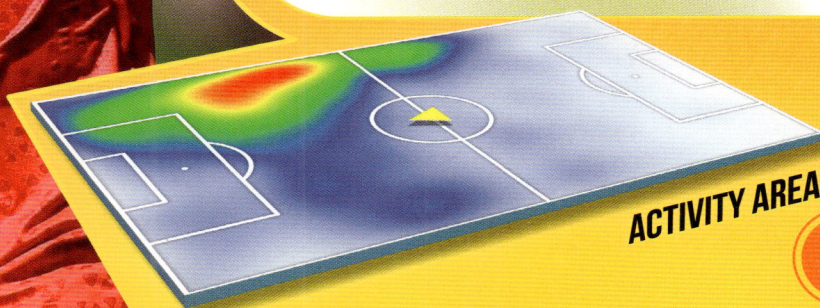

ACTIVITY AREAS

41

CURRENT CLUB
Arsenal

DECLAN RICE

Declan Rice has long been considered an exceptional defensive midfielder; now he has found an attacking flair playing in central midfield. He has added fine ball skills, passing, crossing and long-range shooting to his athleticism and tackling ability.

DATE OF BIRTH	14/01/1999
POSITION	RIGHT
HEIGHT	1.87 M
PRO DEBUT	2017
PREFERRED FOOT	RIGHT

ASSISTS
20

APPEARANCES
273

DRIBBLES
375

PENALTIES SCORED
1

PASSES
13,405

SUCCESSFUL PASSES
88%

GOALS
21

SHOTS
230

CHANCES CREATED
185

TACKLES
608

MAJOR CLUB HONOURS
- Premier League: runner-up 2024
- UEFA Europa Conference League: 2023 (West Ham Utd)

INTERNATIONAL HONOURS
- UEFA European Championship: runner-up 2020 (2021), runner-up 2024
- UEFA Nations League: (third place) 2019

ACTIVITY AREAS

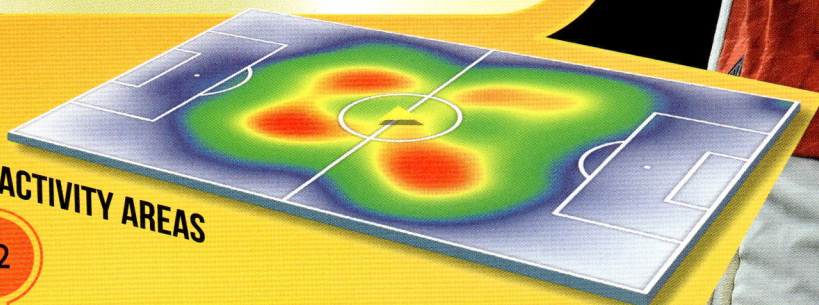

BUKAYO SAKA

A rising star in world football, Buyako Saka's versatility is just one of his talents. Equally good on both sides at full-back or wing-back, his creativity, positional sense, tackling, shooting and passing talents are displayed best as a right midfielder.

NATIONALITY
English

CURRENT CLUB
Arsenal

7

DATE OF BIRTH	05/09/2001
POSITION	WINGER
HEIGHT	1.78 M
PRO DEBUT	2018
PREFERRED FOOT	LEFT

APPEARANCES
204

ASSISTS
47

DRIBBLES
633

PENALTIES SCORED
10

PASSES
6,142
SUCCESSFUL PASSES
82%

GOALS
56

SHOTS
419

CHANCES CREATED
345

TACKLES
268

MAJOR CLUB HONOURS
⚽ Premier League: runner-up 2023, runner-up 2024
⚽ FA Cup: 2020
⚽ UEFA Europa League: runner-up 2019

INTERNATIONAL HONOURS
⚽ UEFA European Championship: runner-up 2020 (2021), runner-up 2024

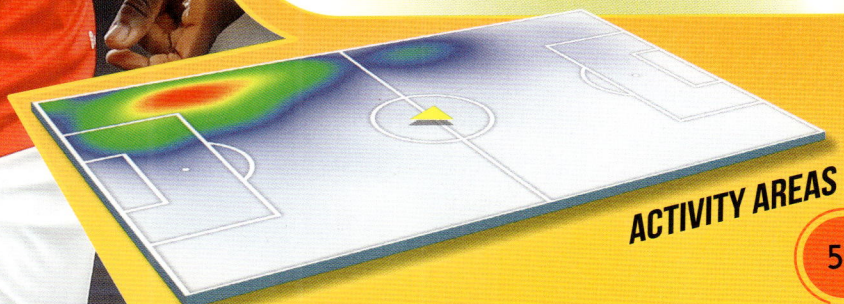

ACTIVITY AREAS

10

NATIONALITY
German

CURRENT CLUB
Bayern Munich

LEROY SANÉ

Leroy Sané is almost the perfect example of a right-winger, except his left foot is stronger. He has all the other attributes to be fearsome on the flanks: great ball control, fine positional and tactical sense, top-class dribbling and outstanding pace to beat defenders.

DATE OF BIRTH	11/01/1996
POSITION	WINGER
HEIGHT	1.83 M
PRO DEBUT	2014
PREFERRED FOOT	LEFT

ASSISTS
85

APPEARANCES
327

DRIBBLES
1,513

PENALTIES SCORED
0

PASSES
9,102
SUCCESSFUL PASSES
83%

GOALS
88

SHOTS
682

CHANCES CREATED
463

TACKLES
343

MAJOR CLUB HONOURS

⊕ Bundesliga: 2021, 2022, 2023 ⊕ FIFA Club World Cup: 2020 2021 ⊕ UEFA Super Cup: 2020 ⊕ Premier League: 2018, 2019 (all Man. City) ⊕ FA Cup: 2019 (Man. City)

INTERNATIONAL HONOURS

⊕ FIFA Confederations Cup: 2017

ACTIVITY AREAS

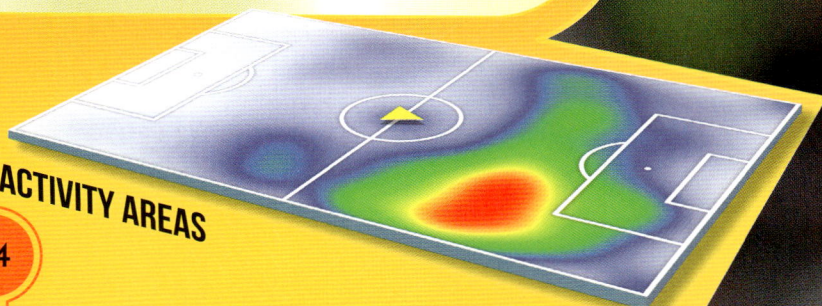

GEORGINIO WIJNALDUM

NATIONALITY
Dutch

CURRENT CLUB
Al-Ittefaq

25

Georginio Wijnaldum can play anywhere in the middle of the pitch as an attacking playmaker or a defensive shield for the back-line. Good with both feet and a strong tackler, he goes box to box and scores crucial goals, especially with headers.

DATE OF BIRTH	11/11/1990
POSITION	CENTRAL
HEIGHT	1.75 M
PRO DEBUT	2007
PREFERRED FOOT	RIGHT

APPEARANCES
589

ASSISTS
48

DRIBBLES
1,075

PASSES
18,310

SUCCESSFUL PASSES
88%

PENALTIES SCORED
6

GOALS
113

SHOTS
776

CHANCES CREATED
458

TACKLES
464

MAJOR CLUB HONOURS
⚽ Ligue 1: 2022 (PSG) ⚽ Premier League: 2020 (Liv'pool)
⚽ UEFA Champions League: 2019 (Liv'pool), runner-up 2018 (Liv'pool) ⚽ Europa League: runner-up 2023 (Roma) ⚽ UEFA Super Cup: 2019 (Liv'pool) ⚽ FIFA Club World Cup: 2019 (Liv'pool)

INTERNATIONAL HONOURS
⚽ UEFA Nations League: runner-up: 2019
⚽ FIFA World Cup: third place 2014

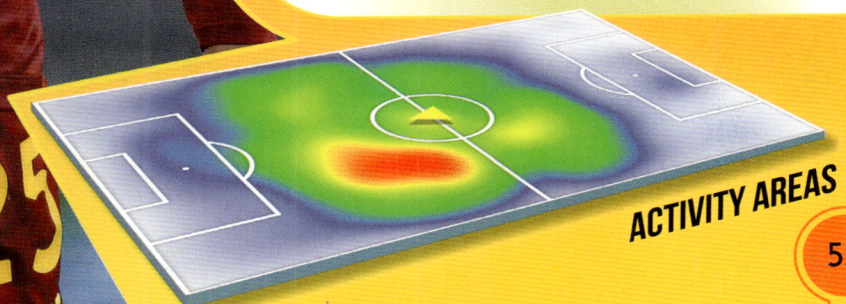

ACTIVITY AREAS

20

NATIONALITY
Belgian

CURRENT CLUB
Atlético Madrid

AXEL WITSEL

Originally a pacey right-winger, Axel Witsel has developed into a strong central midfielder. He frequently drives his team forward with both his play and leadership skills. He is especially good at delivering dangerous passes with either foot.

DATE OF BIRTH	12/01/1989
POSITION	CENTRAL
HEIGHT	1.86 M
PRO DEBUT	2006
PREFERRED FOOT	RIGHT

ASSISTS
11

APPEARANCES
278

DRIBBLES
217

PENALTIES SCORED
1

PASSES
15,193
SUCCESSFUL PASSES
92%

GOALS
21

SHOTS
205

CHANCES CREATED
108

TACKLES
408

MAJOR CLUB HONOURS
⚽ DFL-Pokal: 2021 (Borussia Dortmund)
⚽ DFL-Supercup: 2019 (Borussia Dortmund)

INTERNATIONAL HONOURS
⚽ FIFA World Cup: third place 2018

ACTIVITY AREAS

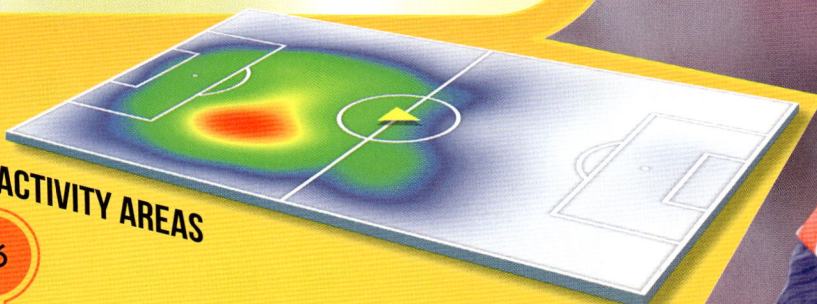

GRANIT XHAKA

Granit Xhaka makes any team he plays for much harder to break down with his performances in defensive midfield. One of the fittest players around, he combines boundless energy with great positional sense and fine tackling technique, and opponents must respect his long-range shooting ability.

NATIONALITY
Swiss

CURRENT CLUB
Bayer Leverkusen

34

DATE OF BIRTH	27/09/1992
POSITION	DEFENSIVE
HEIGHT	1.86 M
PRO DEBUT	2010
PREFERRED FOOT	LEFT

APPEARANCES
451

ASSISTS
34

DRIBBLES
472

PASSES
30,993

SUCCESSFUL PASSES
88%

PENALTIES SCORED
1

GOALS
32

SHOTS
501

CHANCES CREATED
443

TACKLES
798

MAJOR CLUB HONOURS
⚽ Bundesliga: 2024 ⚽ DFB-Pokal: 2024 ⚽ FA Cup: 2017, 2020 (Arsenal) ⚽ Swiss Super League: 2011, 2012 (all Basel)

INTERNATIONAL HONOURS
⚽ None to date

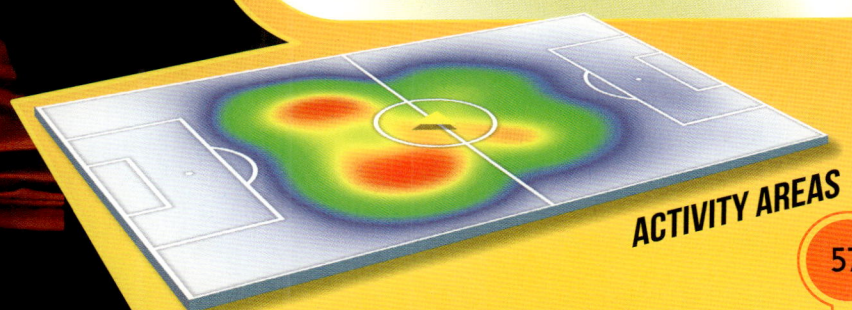

ACTIVITY AREAS

FORWARDS

The forwards are a team's frontline attackers and the chief goalscorers. They are also the team's most celebrated players. Whether it is the smaller, quicker player, such as Neymar and Mohamed Salah, or the bigger, more physical attacker, such as Erling Haaland and Romelu Lukaku, strikers have perfected the art of finding the back of the net on a regular basis. Aside from scoring lots of goals, the world's best strikers are also effective at creating chances for their team-mates.

WHAT DO THE STATS MEAN?

GOALS
This is the total number of goals a striker has scored. The figure spans across all the top clubs the player has represented so far in their career.

ASSISTS
A pass, cross or header to a team-mate who then scores counts as an assist. This stat also includes a deflected shot that is immediately converted by a team-mate.

CONVERSION RATE
75% The percentage shows how good the player is at taking their chance in front of goal. If a player scores two goals from four shots, their conversion rate is 50%.

MINUTES PER GOAL
128 This is the average length of time it takes for the player to score. It is calculated across all the minutes the player has played in their career at top level.

NATIONALITY
French

CURRENT CLUB
Al-Ittihad

KARIM BENZEMA

Karim Benzema, now playing in Saudi Arabia, is an intelligent forward with a great work rate, who can play out wide, down the middle or behind the front man. Although right-footed, he also creates and scores a fair share of goals with his left as well as his head.

DATE OF BIRTH	19/12/1987
POSITION	STRIKER
HEIGHT	1.85 M
PRO DEBUT	2004
PREFERRED FOOT	BOTH

GOALS
380

PENALTIES SCORED
33

ASSISTS
150

APPEARANCES
718

SHOT CONVERSION
18%

MINUTES PER GOAL
137

GOALS LEFT
70

GOALS RIGHT
246

HAT-TRICKS
11

HEADED GOALS
59

SHOTS
2,105

MAJOR CLUB HONOURS

⚽ La Liga: 2012, '17, '20, '22 (R. Madrid) ⚽ UEFA Champions League: 2014, '16, '17, '18, '22 (R. Madrid) ⚽ FIFA Club World Cup: 2014, '16, '17, '18, '22 (R. Madrid) ⚽ UEFA Super Cup: 2014, '16, '17, '22 (R. Madrid) ⚽ Ligue 1: 2005, '06, '07, '08 (Lyon) ⚽ Copa del Rey: 2023 (R. Madrid)

INTERNATIONAL HONOURS

⚽ UEFA Nations League: 2021
⚽ FIFA World Cup: runner-up 2022

ACTIVITY AREAS

JONATHAN DAVID

Jonathan David is a livewire on the pitch who combines speed, balance and excellent ball control. Normally used as second striker, feeding off a target man, he finds holes in opposing defences, through which he can run or deliver inch-perfect passes.

NATIONALITY
Canadian

CURRENT CLUB
Lille

9

DATE OF BIRTH	14/01/2000
POSITION	STRIKER
HEIGHT	1.75 M
PRO DEBUT	2018
PREFERRED FOOT	BOTH

GOALS
77

PENALTIES SCORED
16

ASSISTS
10

APPEARANCES
162

SHOT CONVERSION
22%

MINUTES PER GOAL
158

GOALS LEFT
24

GOALS RIGHT
48

HAT-TRICKS
2

HEADED GOALS
5

SHOTS
343

MAJOR CLUB HONOURS
⚽ Ligue 1: 2021

INTERNATIONAL HONOURS
⚽ None to date

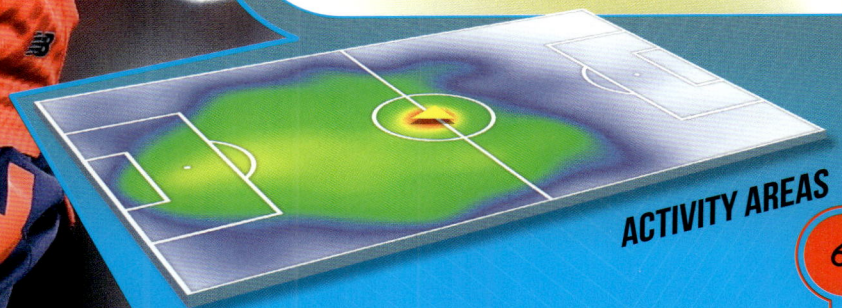

ACTIVITY AREAS

61

MEMPHIS DEPAY

Memphis Depay has developed into a world-class striker, though he is still considered to be a left-winger or left-sided striker. He is a brave player and will challenge the biggest defenders in the middle of the danger area. Depay left Atlético Madrid in 2024 after a single season.

DATE OF BIRTH	13/02/1994
POSITION	WINGER
HEIGHT	1.78 M
PRO DEBUT	2011
PREFERRED FOOT	RIGHT

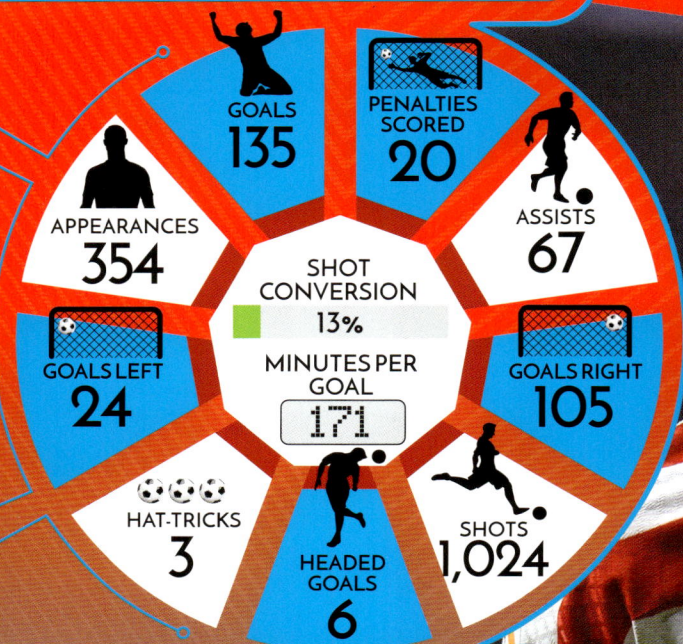

GOALS
135

PENALTIES SCORED
20

ASSISTS
67

APPEARANCES
354

SHOT CONVERSION
13%

MINUTES PER GOAL
171

GOALS LEFT
24

GOALS RIGHT
105

HAT-TRICKS
3

HEADED GOALS
6

SHOTS
1,024

MAJOR CLUB HONOURS

⚽ Eredivisie: 2015 (PSV Eindhoven) ⚽ KNVB Cup: 2012 (PSV Eindhoven) ⚽ FA Cup: 2016 (Manchester United)

INTERNATIONAL HONOURS

⚽ FIFA World Cup: third place 2014

ACTIVITY AREAS

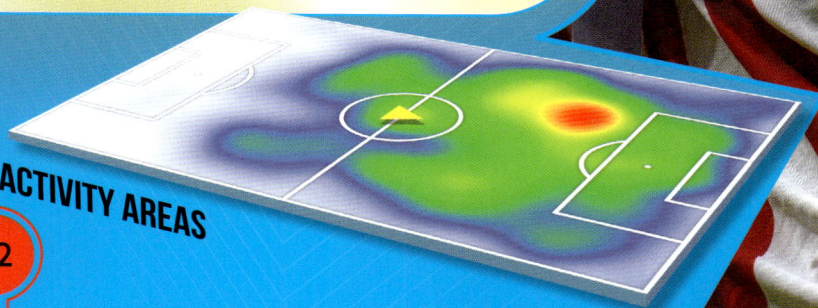

JOÃO FÉLIX

Portugal's João Félix perfected his craft in *La Liga*, where he has now returned following a loan spell in the Premier League in 2023. An eye for goal combined with versatility mean he can be deployed as a central striker, second forward, attacking midfielder or winger.

NATIONALITY
Portuguese

CURRENT CLUB
Barcelona (on loan)

14

DATE OF BIRTH	10/11/1999
PROrposition	
POSITION	FORWARD
HEIGHT	1.81 M
PRO DEBUT	2016
PREFERRED FOOT	RIGHT

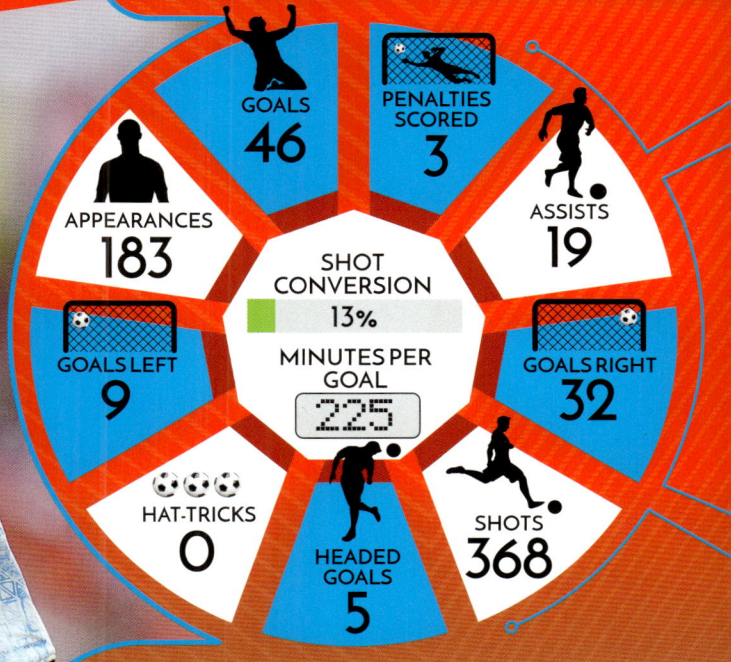

GOALS
46

PENALTIES SCORED
3

APPEARANCES
183

ASSISTS
19

SHOT CONVERSION
13%

MINUTES PER GOAL
225

GOALS LEFT
9

GOALS RIGHT
32

HAT-TRICKS
0

HEADED GOALS
5

SHOTS
368

MAJOR CLUB HONOURS
- La Liga: 2021 (Atlético Madrid)
- Primeira Liga: 2019 (Benfica)

INTERNATIONAL HONOURS
- UEFA Nations League: 2019

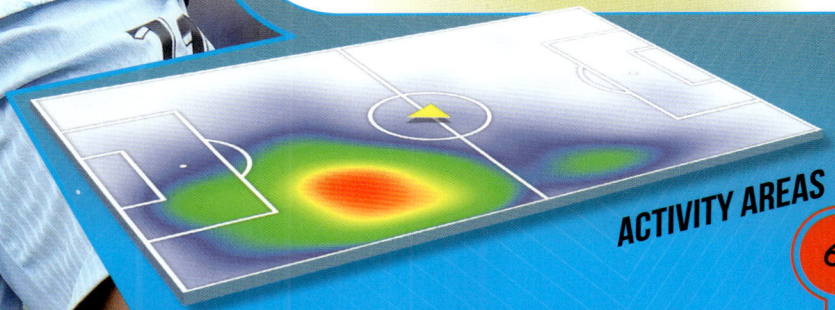

ACTIVITY AREAS

47

NATIONALITY
English

CURRENT CLUB
Manchester City

PHIL FODEN

Phil Foden's meteoric rise may see him become one of the world's best players. Left-footed, he plays on either wing or centrally as a striker or midfielder, where he displays an exceptional first touch, close control, poise, balance, tactical awareness and a powerful shot.

DATE OF BIRTH	28/05/2000
POSITION	SECOND STRIKER
HEIGHT	1.71 M
PRO DEBUT	2016
PREFERRED FOOT	LEFT

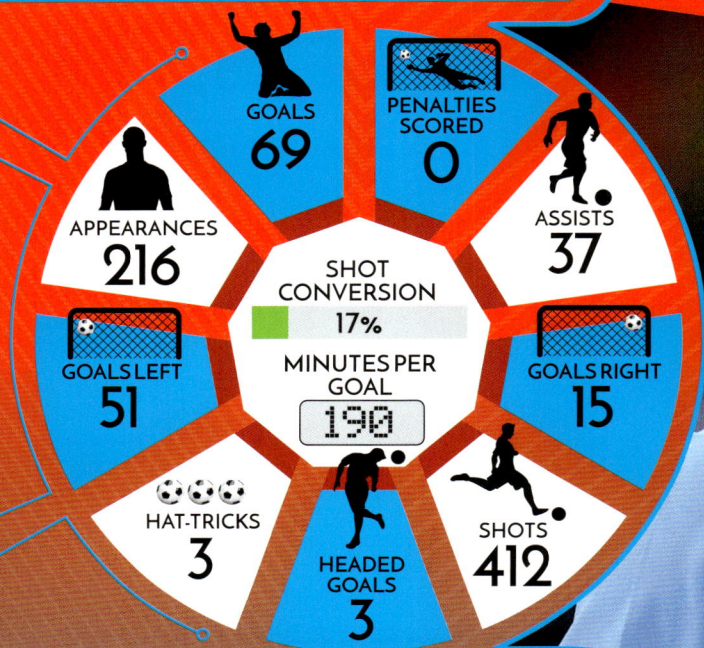

GOALS
69

PENALTIES SCORED
0

APPEARANCES
216

ASSISTS
37

SHOT CONVERSION
17%

MINUTES PER GOAL
190

GOALS LEFT
51

GOALS RIGHT
15

HAT-TRICKS
3

HEADED GOALS
3

SHOTS
412

MAJOR CLUB HONOURS
⚽ Premier League: 2018, 2019, 2021, 2022, 2023, 2024 ⚽ UEFA Champions League: 2023, runners-up 2021 ⚽ UEFA Super Cup: 2023 ⚽ FIFA Club World Cup: 2023 ⚽ FA Cup: 2019, 2023, runner-up 2024

INTERNATIONAL HONOURS
⚽ UEFA European Championship: runner-up 2024

ACTIVITY AREAS

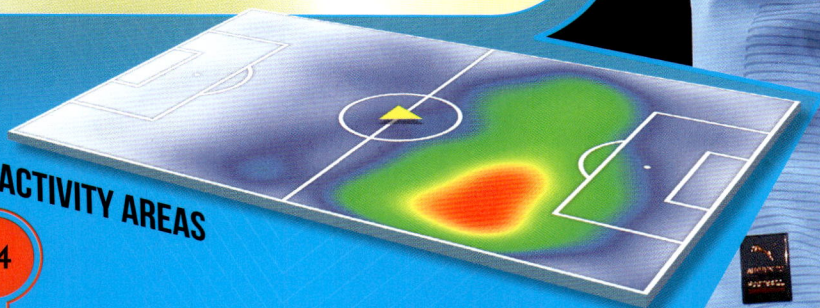

OLIVIER GIROUD

Olivier Giroud is much more than a target man because his work-rate and positional sense make him hard to defend against near the goal. He uses his physique to hold and shield the ball, and is known for his accurate passing, shooting and heading.

NATIONALITY
French

CURRENT CLUB
Los Angeles FC

9

DATE OF BIRTH	30/09/1986
POSITION	STRIKER
HEIGHT	1.93 M
PRO DEBUT	2005
PREFERRED FOOT	LEFT

GOALS
186

PENALTIES SCORED
21

ASSISTS
66

APPEARANCES
489

SHOT CONVERSION
16%

MINUTES PER GOAL
167

GOALS RIGHT
16

GOALS LEFT
112

HAT-TRICKS
6

HEADED GOALS
57

SHOTS
1,173

MAJOR CLUB HONOURS
⚽ Serie A: 2022 (AC Milan) ⚽ UEFA Champions League: 2021 (Chelsea) ⚽ UEFA Europa League: 2019 (Chelsea) ⚽ Ligue 1: 2012 (Montpellier) ⚽ FA Cup: 2014, 2015, 2017 (Arsenal), 2018 (Chelsea)

INTERNATIONAL HONOURS
⚽ FIFA World Cup 2018, runner-up 2022
⚽ UEFA European Championship: runner-up 2016

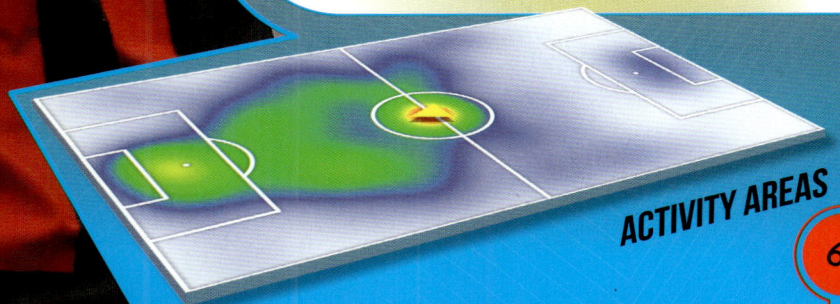

ACTIVITY AREAS

65

NATIONALITY
French

CURRENT CLUB
Atlético Madrid

ANTOINE GRIEZMANN

Known for being the ultimate team player, Antoine Griezmann is able to take on all offensive roles, be it front man, attacking midfielder, false No.9 or coming from wide positions. He is an excellent team-mate, using his experience to improve everyone on the pitch.

DATE OF BIRTH	21/03/1991
POSITION	STRIKER
HEIGHT	1.76 M
PRO DEBUT	2009
PREFERRED FOOT	LEFT

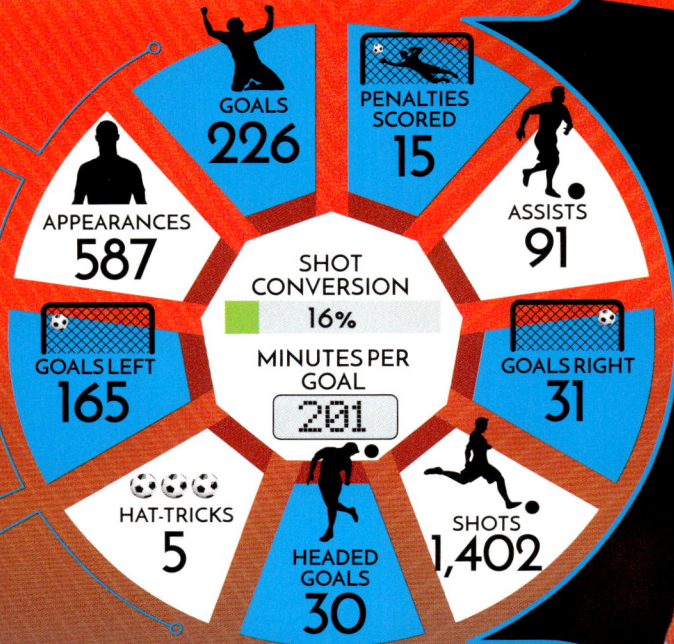

GOALS
226

PENALTIES SCORED
15

ASSISTS
91

APPEARANCES
587

SHOT CONVERSION
16%

MINUTES PER GOAL
201

GOALS LEFT
165

GOALS RIGHT
31

HAT-TRICKS
5

HEADED GOALS
30

SHOTS
1,402

MAJOR CLUB HONOURS
⚽ UEFA Champions League: runner-up 2016
⚽ UEFA Europa League 2018 ⚽ UEFA Super Cup 2018
⚽ Copa del Rey 2021 (Barcelona)

INTERNATIONAL HONOURS
⚽ FIFA World Cup: 2018, runner-up 2022
⚽ UEFA European Championship: runner-up 2016
⚽ UEFA Nations League: 2021

ACTIVITY AREAS

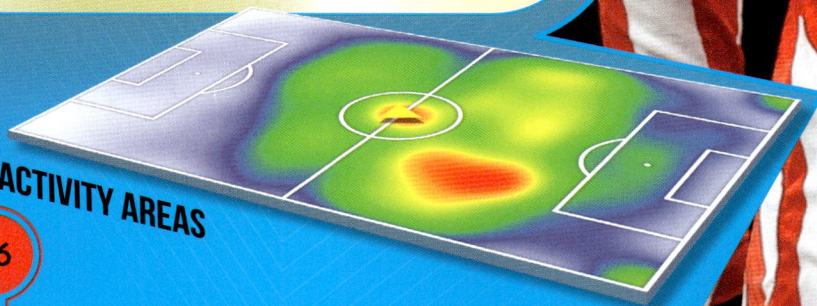

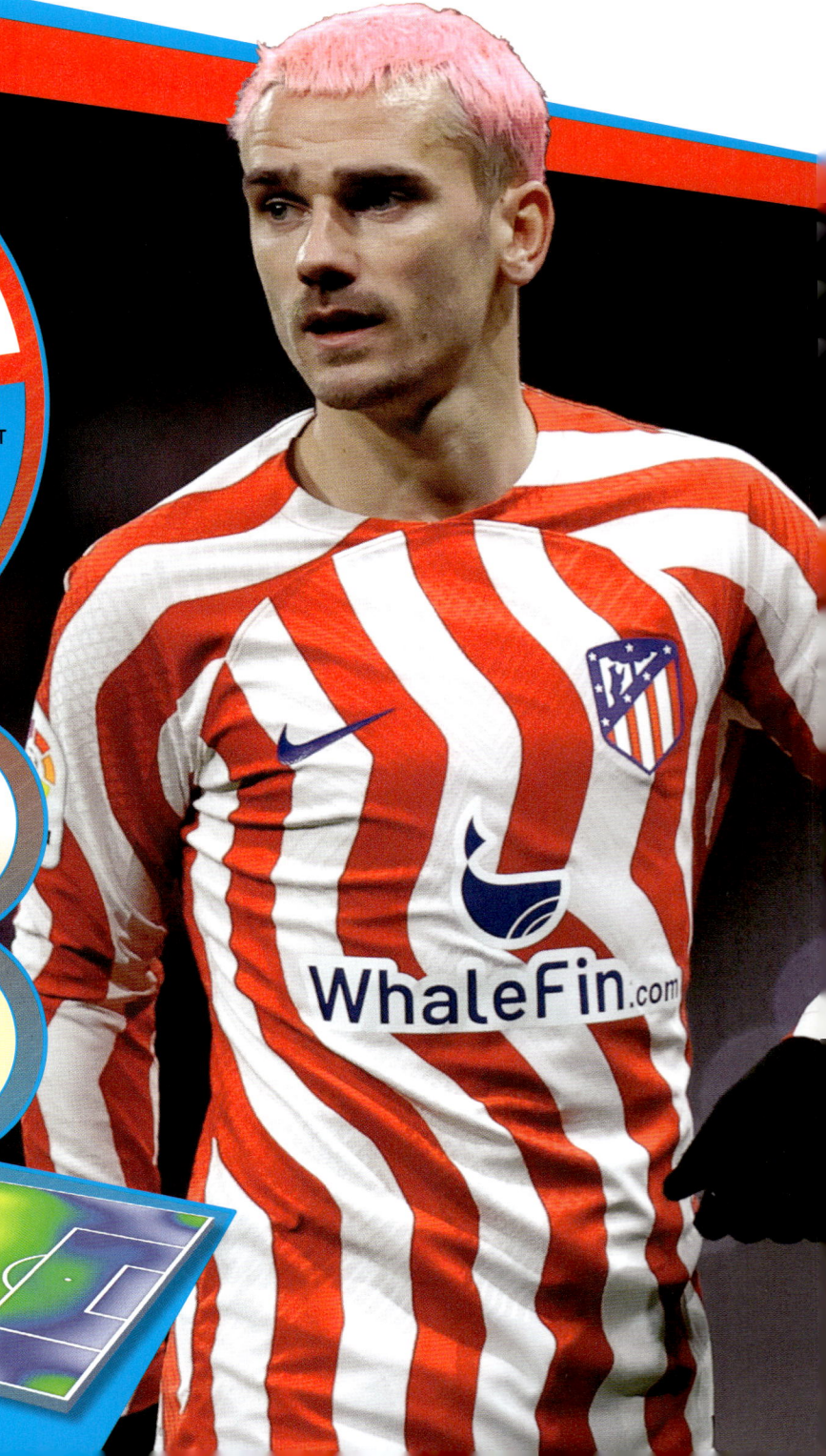

ERLING HAALAND

Erling Haaland has become one of the most exciting forwards in world football. He has all the talents of a world-class striker, including two good feet, blistering pace, the strength to shrug off defenders, aerial dominance and a fearsome predatorial instinct in front of goal.

NATIONALITY
Norwegian

CURRENT CLUB
Manchester City

9

DATE OF BIRTH	21/07/2000
POSITION	STRIKER
HEIGHT	1.94 M
PRO DEBUT	2015
PREFERRED FOOT	LEFT

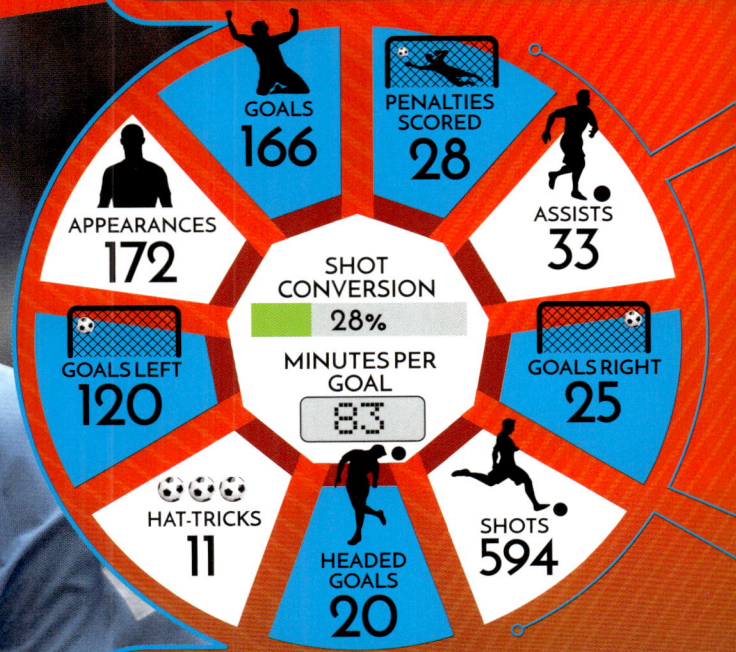

GOALS
166

PENALTIES SCORED
28

ASSISTS
33

APPEARANCES
172

SHOT CONVERSION
28%

MINUTES PER GOAL
83

GOALS LEFT
120

GOALS RIGHT
25

HAT-TRICKS
11

HEADED GOALS
20

SHOTS
594

MAJOR CLUB HONOURS

⚽ Premier League: 2023, 2024 ⚽ UEFA Champions League: 2023 ⚽ DFB-Pokal: 2021 (Borussia Dortmund) ⚽ Austrian Bundesliga: 2019, 2020 (Red Bull Salzburg) ⚽ FA Cup: 2023, runner-up 2024 ⚽ Austrian Cup: 2019 (Red Bull Salzburg)

INTERNATIONAL HONOURS

⚽ None to date

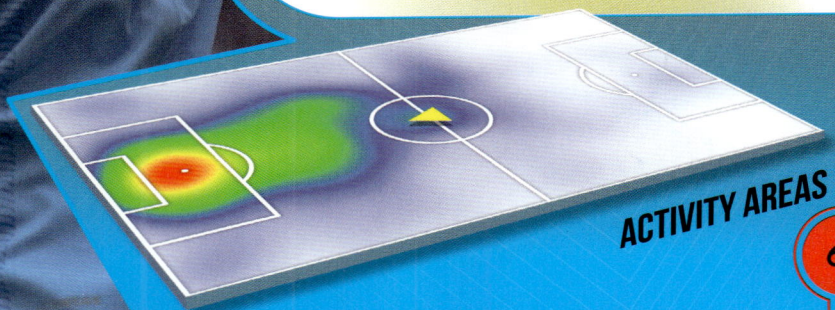

ACTIVITY AREAS

17

NATIONALITY
Italian

CURRENT CLUB
Besiktas

CIRO IMMOBILE

A great team-player, Ciro Immobile is a natural finisher who is excellent in the air. His goals tally is even higher because he refuses to give up lost causes and is willing to chase back to force mistakes out of defenders.

DATE OF BIRTH	20/02/1990
POSITION	STRIKER
HEIGHT	1.85 M
PRO DEBUT	2007
PREFERRED FOOT	RIGHT

GOALS
220

PENALTIES SCORED
56

ASSISTS
51

APPEARANCES
410

SHOT CONVERSION
19%

MINUTES PER GOAL
135

GOALS LEFT
32

GOALS RIGHT
165

HAT-TRICKS
7

HEADED GOALS
23

SHOTS
1,177

MAJOR CLUB HONOURS
⚽ Serie A: Runner-up 2023 (Lazio)
⚽ Coppa Italia: 2019 (Lazio)

INTERNATIONAL HONOURS
✪ UEFA European Championship: 2020
✪ UEFA Nations League: Third place 2023

ACTIVITY AREAS

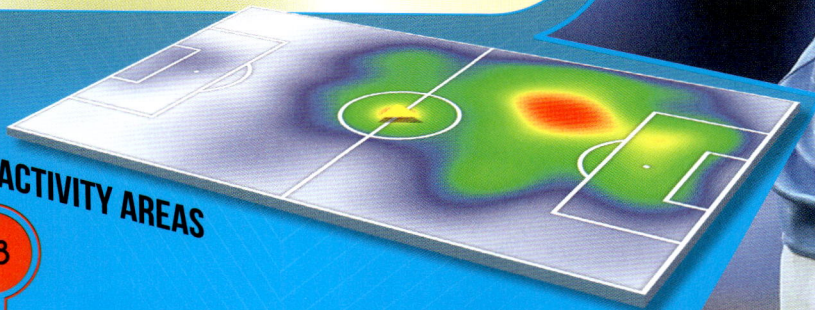

DIOGO JOTA

Although most effective as a main striker, Diogo Jota is able to adapt his game to play deeper or as a left-winger. In this role, he is a master at waiting for defenders to be dragged out of position before running into spaces behind them and shooting powerfully with his right foot.

NATIONALITY
Portuguese

CURRENT CLUB
Liverpool

20

DATE OF BIRTH	04/12/1996
POSITION	STRIKER
HEIGHT	1.78 M
PRO DEBUT	2014
PREFERRED FOOT	RIGHT

GOALS
80

PENALTIES SCORED
1

APPEARANCES
242

ASSISTS
28

SHOT CONVERSION
16%

GOALS LEFT
30

MINUTES PER GOAL
198

GOALS RIGHT
40

HAT-TRICKS
2

HEADED GOALS
10

SHOTS
516

MAJOR CLUB HONOURS
- ⚽ UEFA Champions League: runner-up 2022
- ⚽ FA Cup: 2022
- ⚽ EFL Cup: 2022

INTERNATIONAL HONOURS
- ⚽ UEFA Nations League: 2019

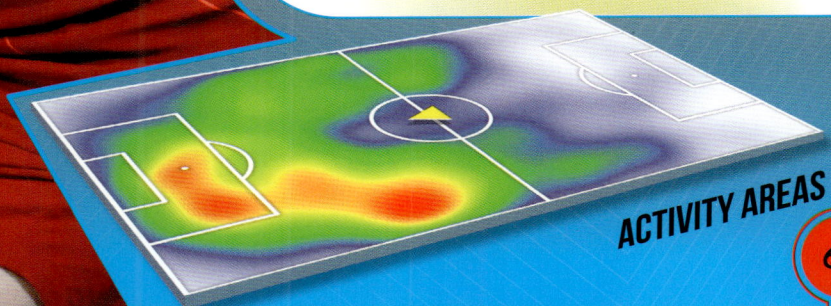

ACTIVITY AREAS

69

15

NATIONALITY
Serbian

CURRENT CLUB
Fiorentina

LUKA JOVIĆ

Luka Jović is a predator in the penalty box. He uses his speed and attacking instincts to find spaces in the penalty area and score goals from close range with deft touches from either foot and occasionally his head.

DATE OF BIRTH	23/12/1997
POSITION	STRIKER
HEIGHT	1.81 M
PRO DEBUT	2014
PREFERRED FOOT	RIGHT

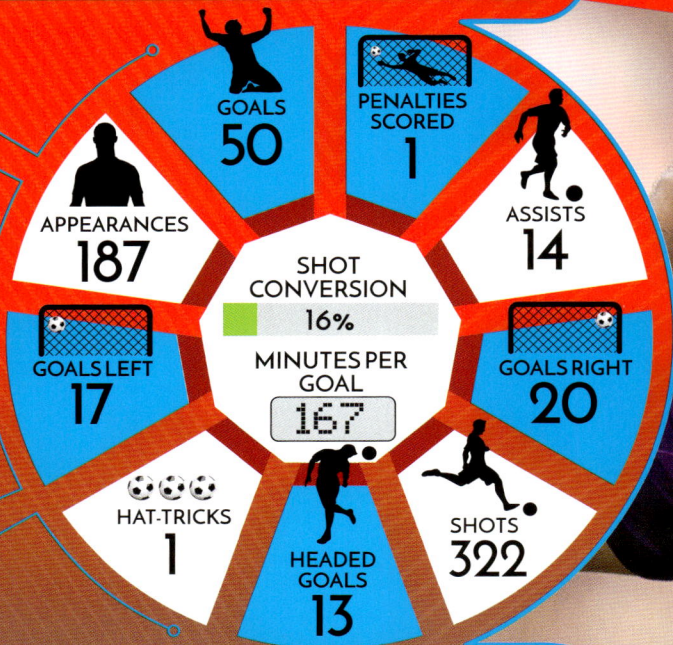

GOALS
50

PENALTIES SCORED
1

ASSISTS
14

APPEARANCES
187

SHOT CONVERSION
16%

MINUTES PER GOAL
167

GOALS RIGHT
20

GOALS LEFT
17

HAT-TRICKS
1

HEADED GOALS
13

SHOTS
322

MAJOR CLUB HONOURS

- ⚽ La Liga: 2020, 2022 (Real Madrid)
- ⚽ UEFA Champions League: 2022 (Real Madrid)
- ⚽ DFB-Pokal: 2018 (Eintracht Frankfurt)

INTERNATIONAL HONOURS

- ⚽ None to date

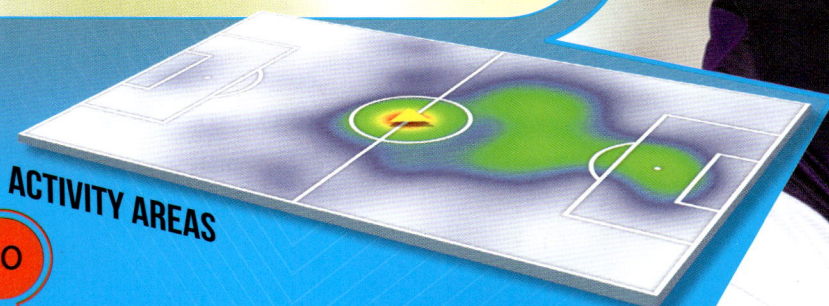

ACTIVITY AREAS

HARRY KANE

Harry Kane has grown into the complete striker. His power in the air, skills with both feet and superb ball-striking technique make him hard to defend against. What's more, with his defence-splitting passes, he also sets up many goals for his team-mates.

DATE OF BIRTH	28/07/1993
POSITION	STRIKER
HEIGHT	1.88 M
PRO DEBUT	2009
PREFERRED FOOT	RIGHT

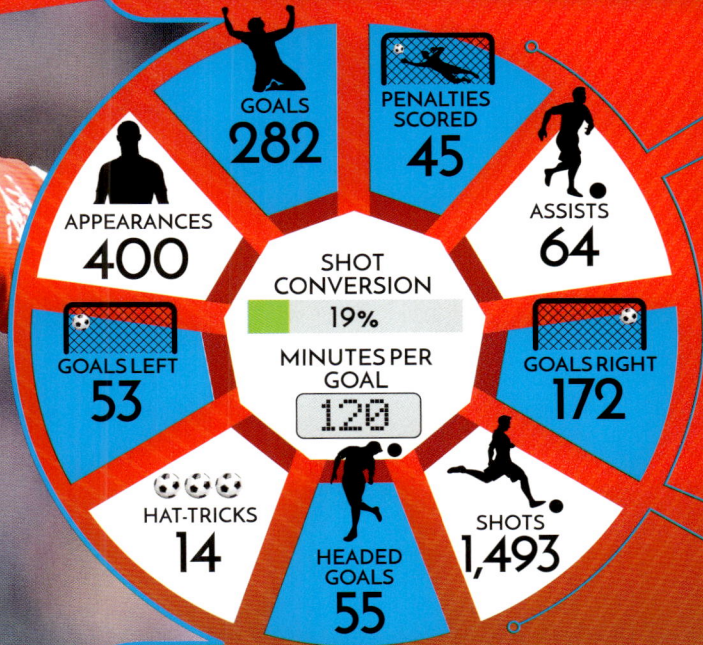

GOALS
282

PENALTIES SCORED
45

APPEARANCES
400

ASSISTS
64

SHOT CONVERSION
19%

GOALS LEFT
53

MINUTES PER GOAL
128

GOALS RIGHT
172

HAT-TRICKS
14

HEADED GOALS
55

SHOTS
1,493

MAJOR CLUB HONOURS
⚽ UEFA Champions League: runner-up 2019 (Tottenham Hotspur)

INTERNATIONAL HONOURS
⚽ UEFA European Championship: runner-up 2020 (2021), runner-up 2024
⚽ UEFA Nations League: third place 2019

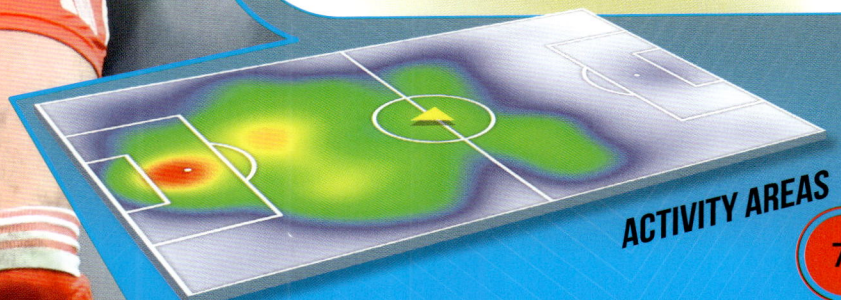

ACTIVITY AREAS

71

ROBERT LEWANDOWSKI

NATIONALITY
Polish

CURRENT CLUB
Barcelona

Robert Lewandowski has consistently ranked as one of the world's best strikers since he made his debut at Borussia Dortmund in 2010. His positioning, technique, power and finishing saw him net more than 300 goals in the Bundesliga before he made his move to Barcelona in 2022.

DATE OF BIRTH	21/08/1988
POSITION	STRIKER
HEIGHT	1.85 M
PRO DEBUT	2005
PREFERRED FOOT	RIGHT

GOALS
448

PENALTIES SCORED
60

APPEARANCES
573

ASSISTS
90

SHOT CONVERSION
20%

MINUTES PER GOAL
105

GOALS LEFT
74

GOALS RIGHT
299

HAT-TRICKS
23

HEADED GOALS
72

SHOTS
2,187

MAJOR CLUB HONOURS

⚽ La Liga: 2023 ⚽ Bundesliga: 2011, 2012 (all B. Dortmund), 2015, '16, '17, '18, '19, '20, '21, '22 (all B. Munich) ⚽ UEFA Champions League: 2020 (B. Munich) ⚽ FIFA Club World Cup: 2020 (B. Munich) ⚽ UEFA Super Cup: 2020 (B. Munich)

INTERNATIONAL HONOURS

⚽ None to date

ACTIVITY AREAS

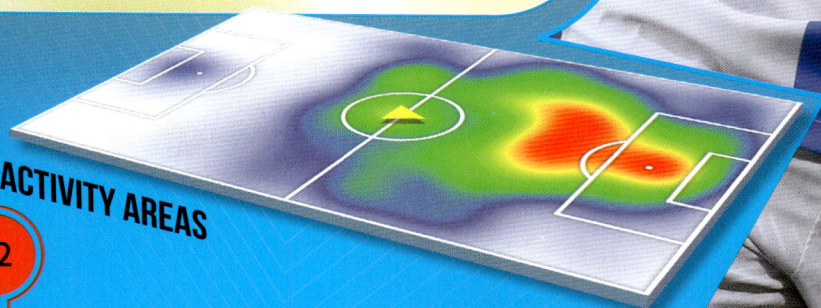

ROMELU LUKAKU

Romelu Lukaku has a breathtaking pace and dribbling ability. Although he normally plays on the wing, he can also be dangerous in the middle of the park as he can leap high to win headers and shoot powerfully with either foot.

NATIONALITY
Belgian

CURRENT CLUB
AS Roma (on loan)

90

DATE OF BIRTH	13/05/1993
POSITION	STRIKER
HEIGHT	1.91 M
PRO DEBUT	2009
PREFERRED FOOT	LEFT

GOALS
209

PENALTIES SCORED
22

ASSISTS
61

APPEARANCES
448

SHOT CONVERSION
19%

MINUTES PER GOAL
160

GOALS LEFT
116

GOALS RIGHT
52

HAT-TRICKS
3

HEADED GOALS
37

SHOTS
1,119

MAJOR CLUB HONOURS

⚽ Serie A: 2021 (Int. Milan) ⚽ UEFA Champions League: runner-up 2023 (Int. Milan) ⚽ Coppa Italia: 2023 (Int. Milan) ⚽ FIFA Club World Cup: 2021 (Chelsea) ⚽ UEFA Europa League: runner-up 2020 (Chelsea) ⚽ Belgian Pro League: 2010 (Anderlecht)

INTERNATIONAL HONOURS

⚽ FIFA World Cup: third place 2018

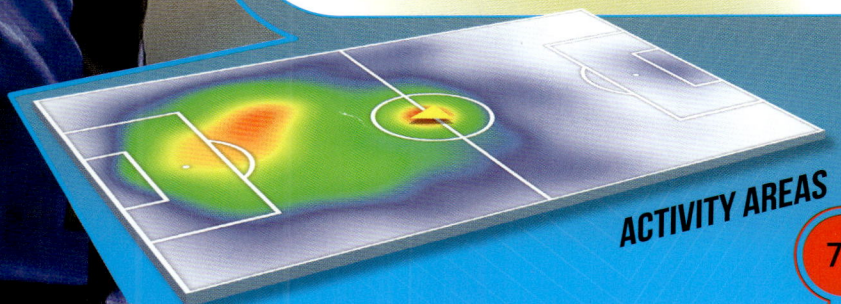

ACTIVITY AREAS

Shirt

9

NATIONALITY
French

CURRENT CLUB
Real Madrid

KYLIAN MBAPPÉ

A FIFA World Cup winner with France at just 18 and a runner-up four years later, Kylian Mbappé is counted among the best strikers in world football today. The pacey finisher is a superb ball-player who consistently gets on the score sheet and sets up chances for his team-mates.

DATE OF BIRTH	20/12/1998
POSITION	STRIKER
HEIGHT	1.78 M
PRO DEBUT	2015
PREFERRED FOOT	RIGHT

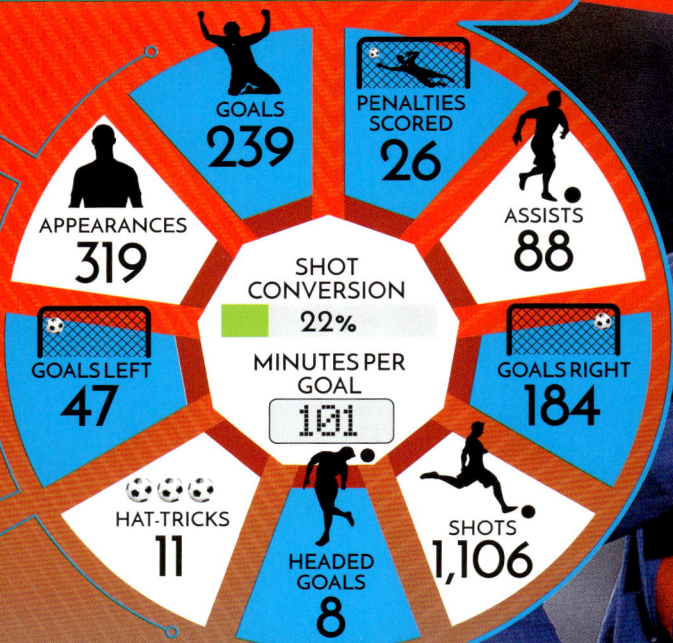

GOALS
239

PENALTIES SCORED
26

APPEARANCES
319

ASSISTS
88

SHOT CONVERSION
22%

MINUTES PER GOAL
101

GOALS LEFT
47

GOALS RIGHT
184

HAT-TRICKS
11

HEADED GOALS
8

SHOTS
1,106

MAJOR CLUB HONOURS
⚽ Ligue 1: 2017 (Monaco), 2018, 2019, 2020, 2022, 2023, 2024 ⚽ UEFA Champions League: runner-up 2020
⚽ Coupe de France: 2018, 2020, 2021, 2024

INTERNATIONAL HONOURS
⚽ FIFA World Cup: 2018, runner-up 2022
⚽ UEFA Nations League: 2021

ACTIVITY AREAS

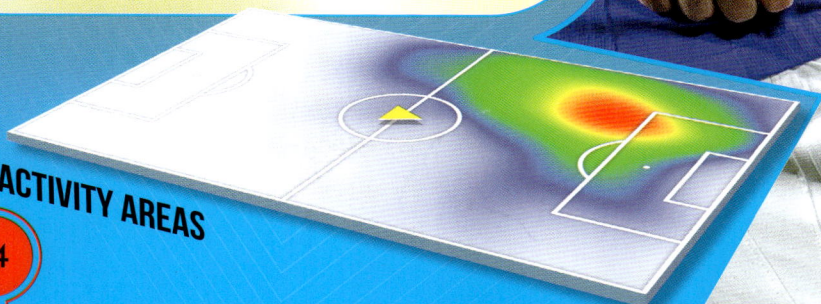

74

LIONEL MESSI

The greatest player of his generation, if not the greatest ever, the 2022 World Cup winner is a fine playmaker with a stunning goal-scoring record. He is also a fantastically fast dribbler who can carve out opportunities to shoot with either foot, from any range and rarely misses the target.

NATIONALITY
Argentinian

CURRENT CLUB
Inter Miami

10

DATE OF BIRTH	24/06/1987
POSITION	FORWARD
HEIGHT	1.70 M
PRO DEBUT	2003
PREFERRED FOOT	LEFT

GOALS
637

PENALTIES SCORED
79

APPEARANCES
751

ASSISTS
272

SHOT CONVERSION
19%

MINUTES PER GOAL
97

GOALS LEFT
529

GOALS RIGHT
85

HAT-TRICKS
44

HEADED GOALS
21

SHOTS
3,370

MAJOR CLUB HONOURS

⚽ Ligue 1: 2022, 2023 (PSG) ⚽ La Liga: 2005, '06, '09, '10 '11, '13, '15, '16, '18, '19 (all Barça) ⚽ UEFA Champions League: 2006, '09, '11, '15 (all Barça) ⚽ UEFA Super Cup: 2009, '11, '15 (all Barça) ⚽ FIFA Club World Cup: 2009, '11, '15 (all Barça) ⚽ MLS Leagues Cup: 2023

INTERNATIONAL HONOURS

⚽ FIFA World Cup: 2022, runner-up 2014
⚽ Olympic Games: gold medal 2008
⚽ Copa América: 2021, 2024, runner-up* 2007*, 2015*, 2016*

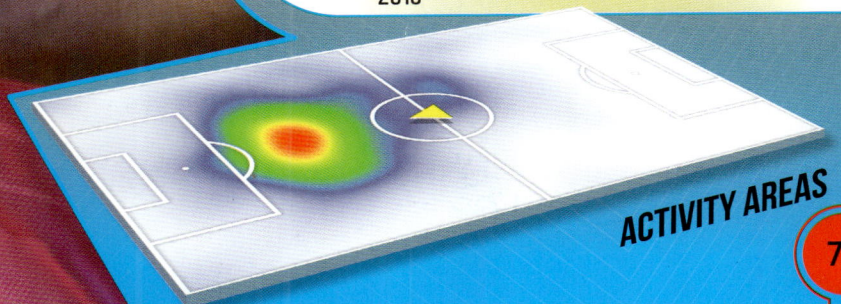

ACTIVITY AREAS

ÁLVARO MORATA

NATIONALITY
Spanish

CURRENT CLUB
AC Milan

7

Álvaro Morata is perfectly built for a central striker. Tall, strong and excellent in the air, he is comfortable with the ball at his feet. Morata is also surprisingly fast and has great tactical and positional awareness.

DATE OF BIRTH	23/10/1992
POSITION	STRIKER
HEIGHT	1.90 M
PRO DEBUT	2010
PREFERRED FOOT	RIGHT

GOALS
150

PENALTIES SCORED
5

ASSISTS
55

APPEARANCES
439

SHOT CONVERSION
18%

MINUTES PER GOAL
161

GOALS LEFT
38

GOALS RIGHT
74

HAT-TRICKS
3

HEADED GOALS
38

SHOTS
838

MAJOR CLUB HONOURS
⚽ La Liga: 2012, 2017 (R. Madrid)　⚽ Serie A: 2015, 2016 (all Juventus)
⚽ UEFA Champions League: 2014, '17 (R. Madrid), runner-up 2015 (Juventus)
⚽ UEFA Europa League: 2019 (Chelsea)　⚽ UEFA Super Cup: 2016 (R. Madrid)
⚽ FIFA Club World Cup: 2016 (R. Madrid)

INTERNATIONAL HONOURS
⚽ UEFA European Championship: 2024
⚽ UEFA Nations League: 2023
⚽ UEFA European U-21 Championship: 2013

ACTIVITY AREAS

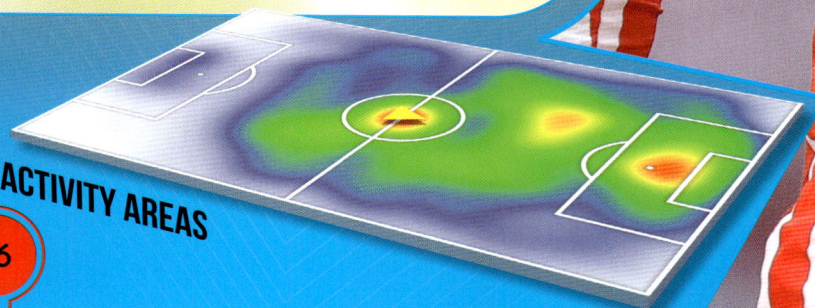

NEYMAR

Counted among the long line of great Brazilian strikers to become a superstar, Neymar moved to the Saudi Pro League in 2023. His pace and phenomenal dribbling help him beat defenders in numbers. He strikes fear into the opposition defence with his energetic pace and playmaking skills.

NATIONALITY
Brazilian

CURRENT CLUB
Al Hilal

10

DATE OF BIRTH	05/02/1992
POSITION	FORWARD
HEIGHT	1.75 M
PRO DEBUT	2009
PREFERRED FOOT	RIGHT

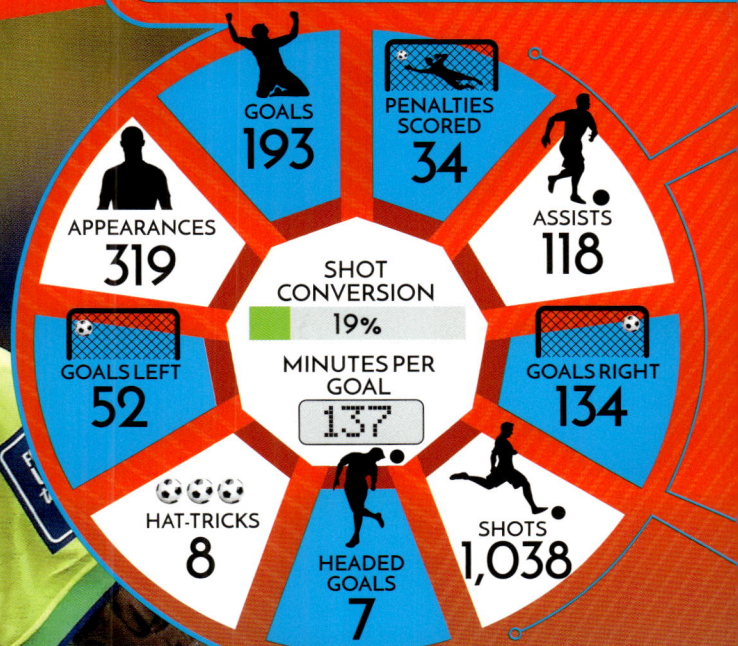

GOALS
193

PENALTIES SCORED
34

ASSISTS
118

APPEARANCES
319

SHOT CONVERSION
19%

MINUTES PER GOAL
137

GOALS LEFT
52

GOALS RIGHT
134

HAT-TRICKS
8

HEADED GOALS
7

SHOTS
1,038

MAJOR CLUB HONOURS
⚽ La Liga: 2015, '16, '17 (all Barça) ⚽ Ligue 1: 2018, '19 '20, 2022, 2023 (all PSG) ⚽ UEFA Champions League: 2016 (Barça) ⚽ FIFA Club World Cup: 2016 (Barça) ⚽ Copa del Rey: 2015, '16, '17 (all Barça) ⚽ Coupe de France: 2018, '20, '21 (all PSG)

INTERNATIONAL HONOURS
⚽ Copa América: runner-up 2021
⚽ FIFA Confederations Cup: 2013
⚽ Olympic Games: silver medal 2012, gold medal 2016

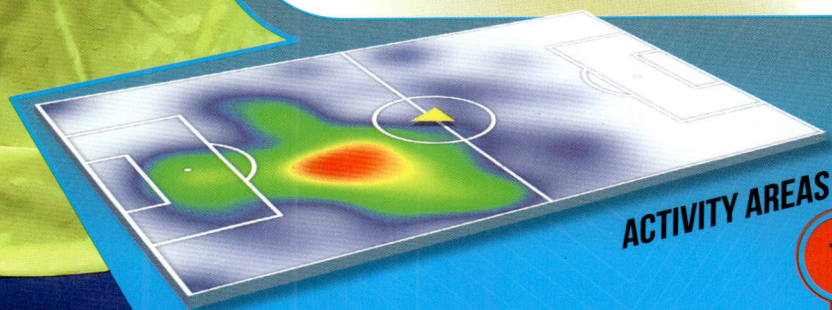

ACTIVITY AREAS

10

NATIONALITY
English

CURRENT CLUB
Manchester United

MARCUS RASHFORD

A great player to watch when he is on form, Marcus Rashford has scored some stunning goals for both club and country. He prefers to raid from the left side, to be on his stronger right foot, but his pace and heading ability make him just as dangerous in the middle.

DATE OF BIRTH	31/10/1997
POSITION	FORWARD
HEIGHT	1.80 M
PRO DEBUT	2015
PREFERRED FOOT	RIGHT

GOALS
95

PENALTIES SCORED
10

ASSISTS
42

APPEARANCES
305

SHOT CONVERSION
15%

MINUTES PER GOAL
218

GOALS LEFT
12

GOALS RIGHT
75

HAT-TRICKS
1

HEADED GOALS
8

SHOTS
653

MAJOR CLUB HONOURS
- UEFA Europa League: 2017, runner-up 2021
- FA Cup: 2016, runner-up 2023, 2024
- EFL Cup: 2023

INTERNATIONAL HONOURS
- UEFA European Championship: runner-up 2021
- UEFA Nations League: third place 2019

ACTIVITY AREAS

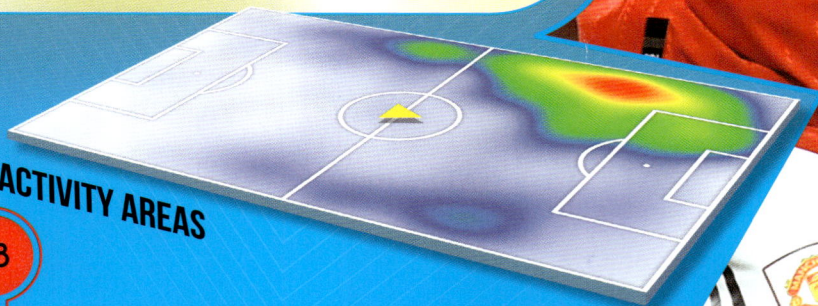

MARCO REUS

Marco Reus is an attacker who can lead the front line, play as a second striker or out wide. He is an expert finisher, especially with his right foot, and is also fantastic at setting up chances for his team-mates. Reus parted ways with Dortmund in 2024 after serving the club for 12 seasons.

NATIONALITY
German

CURRENT CLUB
TBC

DATE OF BIRTH	31/05/1989
POSITION	FORWARD
HEIGHT	1.80 M
PRO DEBUT	2006
PREFERRED FOOT	RIGHT

GOALS
180

PENALTIES SCORED
18

ASSISTS
108

APPEARANCES
463

SHOT CONVERSION
17%

MINUTES PER GOAL
195

GOALS LEFT
43

GOALS RIGHT
131

HAT-TRICKS
3

HEADED GOALS
6

SHOTS
1,080

MAJOR CLUB HONOURS

⚽ Bundesliga: runner-up 2023 (B. Dortmund) ⚽ UEFA Champions League: runner-up 2013 (B. Dortmund), runner-up 2024 (B. Dortmund) ⚽ DFB-Pokal: 2017, 2021, runner-up* 2014*, 2015*, 2016* (all B. Dortmund)

INTERNATIONAL HONOURS

⚽ None to date

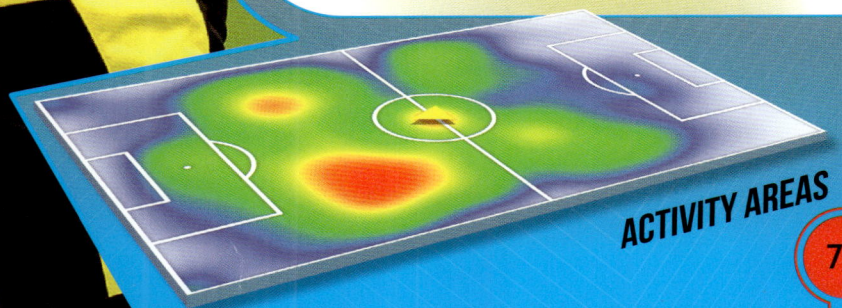

ACTIVITY AREAS

7

NATIONALITY
Portuguese

CURRENT CLUB
Al Nassr

CRISTIANO RONALDO

The superstar striker — now playing in Saudi Arabia — has wowed fans across the world with his all-around attacking skills. He is breathtaking to watch when he is running at defenses, brilliant in the air, and a superb finisher with an extraordinary goal-scoring record.

DATE OF BIRTH	05/02/1985
POSITION	FORWARD
HEIGHT	1.88 M
PRO DEBUT	2002
PREFERRED FOOT	RIGHT

GOALS **675**

PENALTIES SCORED **130**

ASSISTS **184**

APPEARANCES **782**

SHOT CONVERSION **15%**

MINUTES PER GOAL **98**

GOALS LEFT **116**

GOALS RIGHT **449**

HAT-TRICKS **53**

HEADED GOALS **108**

SHOTS **4,556**

MAJOR CLUB HONOURS

⚽ UEFA Champions League: 2008 (Man. U), 2014, '16, '17, '18 (R. Madrid) ⚽ FIFA Club World Cup: 2008 (Man. U), 2014, '16, '17 (R. Madrid) ⚽ UEFA Super Cup: 2014, '17 (R. Madrid) ⚽ Serie A: 2019, '20 (Juventus) ⚽ Premier League: 2007, '08, '09 (Man. U) ⚽ La Liga: 2012, '17 (R. Madrid)

INTERNATIONAL HONOURS

⚽ UEFA European Championship: 2016
⚽ UEFA Nations League: 2019

ACTIVITY AREAS

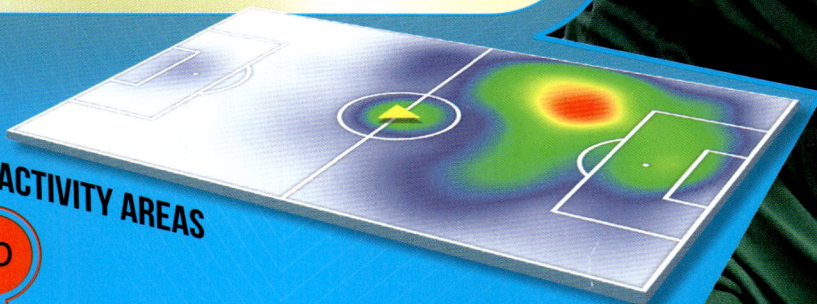

MOHAMED SALAH

The two-time African Footballer Of The Year is a brilliant left-footed attacker who prowls the left wing. Mo Salah has amazing pace with the ability to make angled runs, finding gaps in defences before scoring spectacular goals.

NATIONALITY
Egyptian

CURRENT CLUB
Liverpool

11

DATE OF BIRTH	15/06/1992
POSITION	WINGER
HEIGHT	1.75 M
PRO DEBUT	2010
PREFERRED FOOT	LEFT

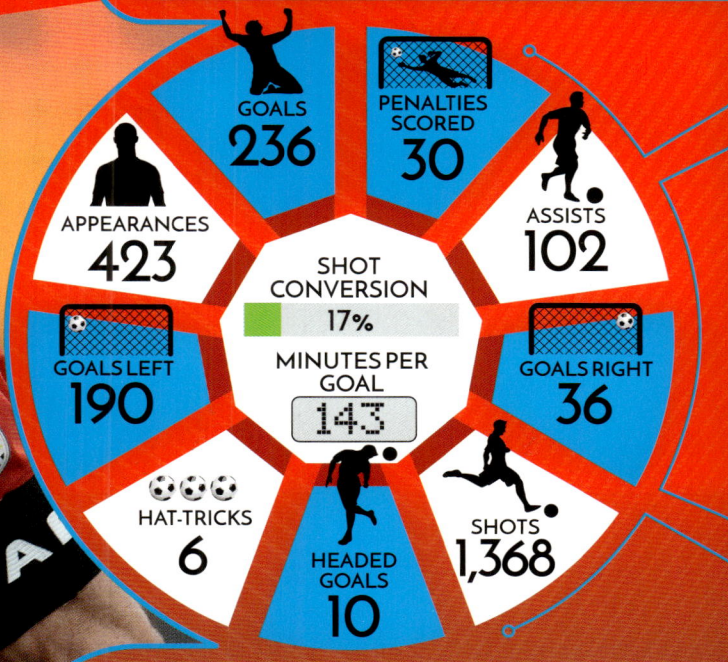

GOALS
236

PENALTIES SCORED
30

APPEARANCES
423

ASSISTS
102

SHOT CONVERSION
17%

MINUTES PER GOAL
143

GOALS LEFT
190

GOALS RIGHT
36

HAT-TRICKS
6

HEADED GOALS
10

SHOTS
1,368

MAJOR CLUB HONOURS
⚽ Premier League: 2020 ⚽ UEFA Champions League: 2019, runner-up 2018, runner-up 2022 ⚽ UEFA Super Cup: 2019 ⚽ FIFA Club World Cup: 2019 ⚽ FA Cup: 2022

INTERNATIONAL HONOURS
⚽ CAF Africa Cup of Nations: runner-up 2017, runner-up 2021

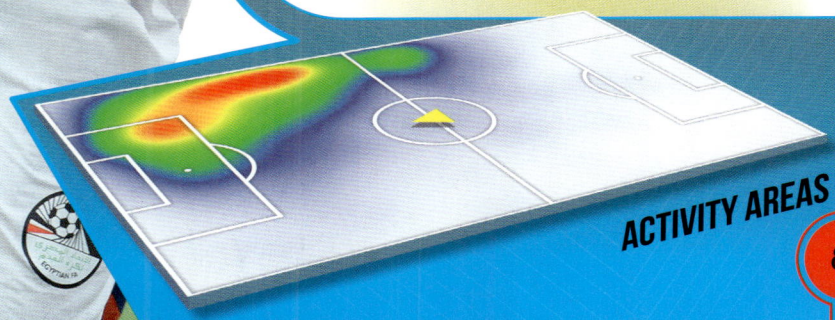

ACTIVITY AREAS

81

7

NATIONALITY
South Korean

CURRENT CLUB
Tottenham Hotspur

SON HEUNG-MIN

Son Heung-Min is at his best when he plays behind the main striker. Although excellent with both feet, attacking from the right side is his strength and he converts a lot of chances that are set up by knock-downs or passes across the box.

DATE OF BIRTH	08/07/1992
POSITION	WINGER
HEIGHT	1.84 M
PRO DEBUT	2010
PREFERRED FOOT	BOTH

GOALS
181

PENALTIES SCORED
3

APPEARANCES
496

ASSISTS
75

SHOT CONVERSION
17%

MINUTES PER GOAL
195

GOALS LEFT
70

GOALS RIGHT
102

HAT-TRICKS
6

HEADED GOALS
9

SHOTS
1,091

MAJOR CLUB HONOURS
⚽ UEFA Champions League: runner-up 2019

INTERNATIONAL HONOURS
⚽ AFC Asian Cup: runner-up 2015

ACTIVITY AREAS

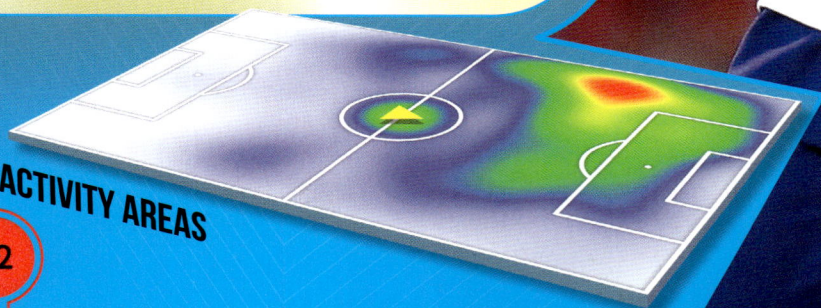

VINÍCIUS JÚNIOR

Vinícius Júnior loves terrorising right-backs, attacking off the left flank, cutting inside to deliver crosses or shooting with his favoured right foot. He brings flair and panache, combined with blistering pace and fantastic dribbling, making him truly world class on his day.

NATIONALITY
Brazilian

CURRENT CLUB
Real Madrid

DATE OF BIRTH	12/07/2000
POSITION	WINGER
HEIGHT	1.76 M
PRO DEBUT	2017
PREFERRED FOOT	RIGHT

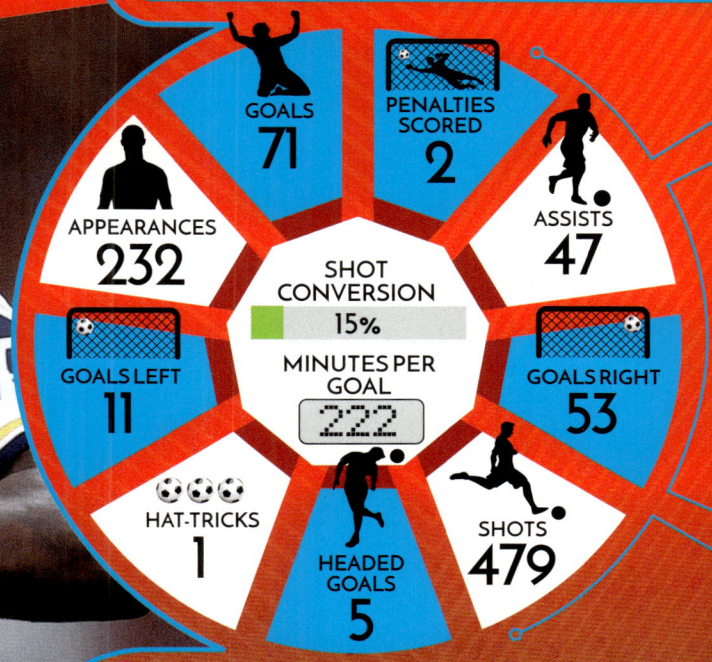

GOALS
71

PENALTIES SCORED
2

ASSISTS
47

APPEARANCES
232

SHOT CONVERSION
15%

MINUTES PER GOAL
222

GOALS LEFT
11

GOALS RIGHT
53

HAT-TRICKS
1

HEADED GOALS
5

SHOTS
479

MAJOR CLUB HONOURS
⚽ UEFA Champions League: 2022, 2024 ⚽ La Liga: 2020, 2022, 2024 ⚽ FIFA Club World Cup: 2018, 2022 ⚽ UEFA Super Cup: 2022 ⚽ Copa del Rey: 2023

INTERNATIONAL HONOURS
⚽ None to date

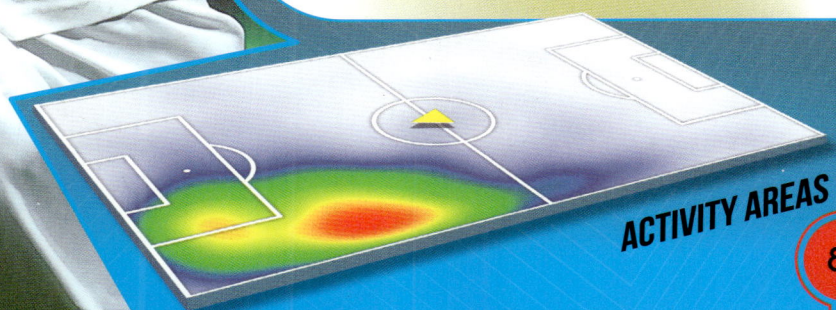

ACTIVITY AREAS

GOALKEEPERS

The goalkeeper is a team's last line of defence and, unlike the other positions, there is no one playing next to them. There is more pressure on goalkeepers than in any other position because when a keeper makes an error, the chances are that the other team will score. The goalies featured in this section are all great shot-stoppers, but some play outside their penalty areas as sweeper-keepers; others have made their reputation as penalty-savers; then there are those who are great at catching the ball or punching it clear.

WHAT DO THE STATS MEAN?

CATCHES
This is the number of times the keeper has dealt with an attack – usually a cross – by catching the ball.

CLEAN SHEETS
Any occasion on which the goalie has not let in a goal for the full duration of the game counts as a clean sheet.

GOALS CONCEDED
This is the number of goals the keeper has conceded in their career in top-division football.

PENALTIES FACED/SAVED
This is the number of times a goalie has faced a penalty (excludes shoot-outs) and how successful he has been at saving it.

PUNCHES
This is a measure of how often the keeper has dealt with a dangerous ball (usually a cross) by punching it clear.

SAVES
This shows how many times the goalkeeper has stopped a shot or header that was on target.

Goalkeepers can, in theory, score goals with their hands. If they throw a ball downfield and it goes directly into the opposition net, the goal will count but, of course, the ball would have to travel 90+ metres, which is unlikely.

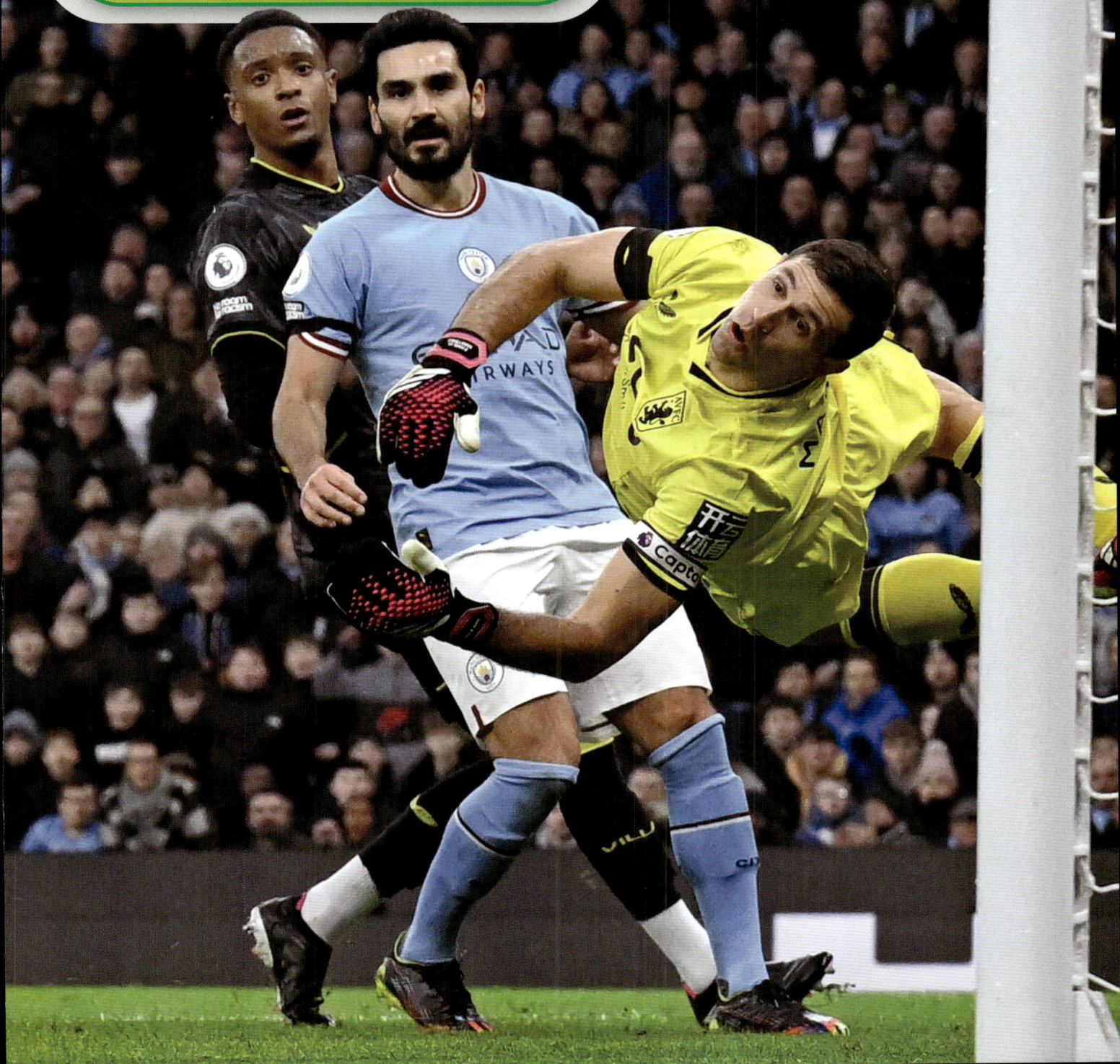

1

NATIONALITY
Brazilian

CURRENT CLUB
Liverpool

ALISSON

The Brazilian has proved to be a top keeper at Liverpool. Alisson is a superb shot-stopper and great at dealing with crosses. Incredibly quick off his line to foil any threat, he can turn defence into attack by finding team-mates with long or short passes.

DATE OF BIRTH	02/10/1992
POSITION	GOALKEEPER
HEIGHT	1.93 M
PRO DEBUT	2013
PREFERRED FOOT	RIGHT

GOALS CONCEDED
281

APPEARANCES
308

PENALTIES SAVED
5

CLEAN SHEETS
132

SAVES
793

PENALTIES FACED
22

CATCHES
136

PUNCHES
119

MAJOR CLUB HONOURS
⚽ Premier League: 2020
⚽ UEFA Champions League: 2019, runner-up 2022
⚽ FIFA Club World Cup: 2019
⚽ FA Cup: 2022

INTERNATIONAL HONOURS
⚽ Copa América: 2019, runner-up 2021

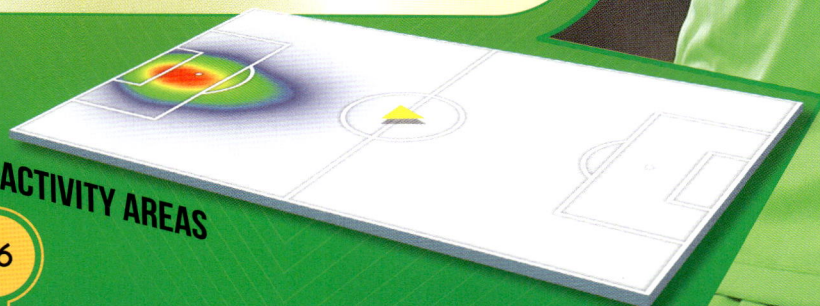

ACTIVITY AREAS

CLAUDIO BRAVO

Claudio Bravo is an accomplished presence in goal with high levels of composure and concentration. As well as being comfortable with the ball at his feet and a good distributor, he is a great shot-stopper, especially when facing penalty kicks. Bravo left Real Betis in 2024 after four seasons.

NATIONALITY
Chilean

CURRENT CLUB
TBC

1

DATE OF BIRTH	13/04/1983
POSITION	GOALKEEPER
HEIGHT	1.84 M
PRO DEBUT	2002
PREFERRED FOOT	RIGHT

GOALS CONCEDED
407

APPEARANCES
351

PENALTIES SAVED
6

SAVES
996

CLEAN SHEETS
117

PENALTIES FACED
33

CATCHES
360

PUNCHES
159

MAJOR CLUB HONOURS
⚽ UEFA Champions League: 2015 (Barcelona) ⚽ La Liga: 2015, 2016 (Barcelona) ⚽ Premier League: 2018 (Man. City) ⚽ FIFA Club World Cup: 2015 (Barcelona) ⚽ UEFA Super Cup: 2015 (Barcelona)

INTERNATIONAL HONOURS
⚽ Copa América: 2015, 2016 ⚽ FIFA Confederations Cup: runner-up 2017

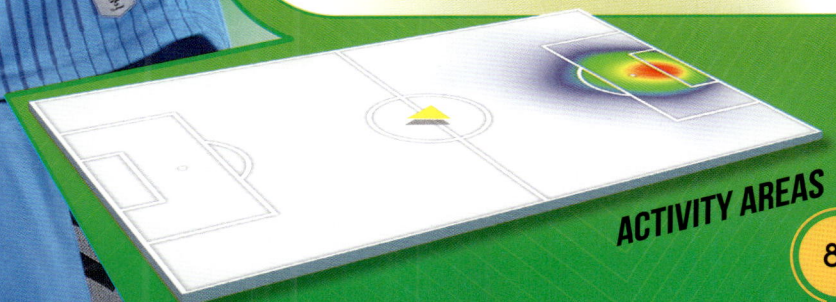

ACTIVITY AREAS

NATIONALITY
Belgian

CURRENT CLUB
Real Madrid

THIBAUT COURTOIS

Thibaut Courtois uses his height to dominate his penalty area, catching crosses and punching well. An agile shot-stopper, he can get down low to make saves, communicates well with his defence, is excellent coming off his line and passes well.

DATE OF BIRTH	11/05/1992
POSITION	GOALKEEPER
HEIGHT	1.99 M
PRO DEBUT	2009
PREFERRED FOOT	LEFT

GOALS CONCEDED
454

APPEARANCES
497

PENALTIES SAVED
8

SAVES
1,257

CLEAN SHEETS
211

PENALTIES FACED
44

PUNCHES
144

CATCHES
505

MAJOR CLUB HONOURS
⚽ La Liga: 2014 (Atlético. Madrid), 2020, 2022, runner-up 2023, 2024 ⚽ Prem. League: 2015, 2017 (all Chelsea) ⚽ UEFA Champions League: 2022, 2024 ⚽ UEFA Europa League: 2012 (Atlético Madrid) ⚽ FIFA Club World Cup: 2018 ⚽ UEFA Super Cup: 2012 (Atlético Madrid) 2022

INTERNATIONAL HONOURS
⚽ FIFA World Cup: third place 2018

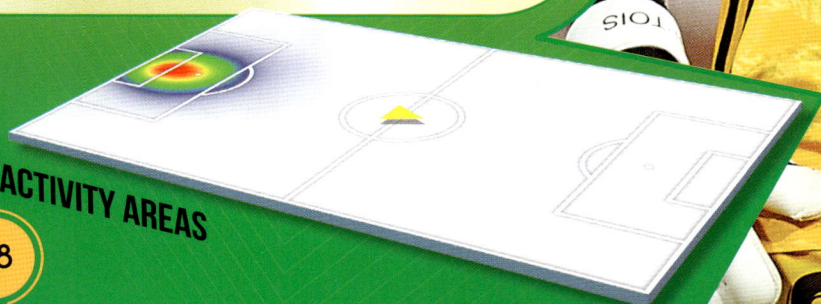

ACTIVITY AREAS

GIANLUIGI DONNARUMMA

The Italian is an amazing talent who made his Serie A debut aged just 16, won his first Italian cap at 17 and became a European champion at 22. Mentally strong and composed under pressure, he has everything it takes to become an all-time great.

NATIONALITY
Italian

CURRENT CLUB
Paris Saint-Germain

99

DATE OF BIRTH	25/02/1999
POSITION	GOALKEEPER
HEIGHT	1.96 M
PRO DEBUT	2015
PREFERRED FOOT	RIGHT

GOALS CONCEDED
356

APPEARANCES
336

PENALTIES SAVED
11

CLEAN SHEETS
107

SAVES
998

PENALTIES FACED
49

CATCHES
207

PUNCHES
154

MAJOR CLUB HONOURS
- Ligue 1: 2022, 2023, 2024
- Coupe de France: 2024
- Supercoppa Italiana: 2016 (AC Milan)

INTERNATIONAL HONOURS
- UEFA European Championship: 2020 (2021)
- UEFA Nations League: third place 2021, third place 2023

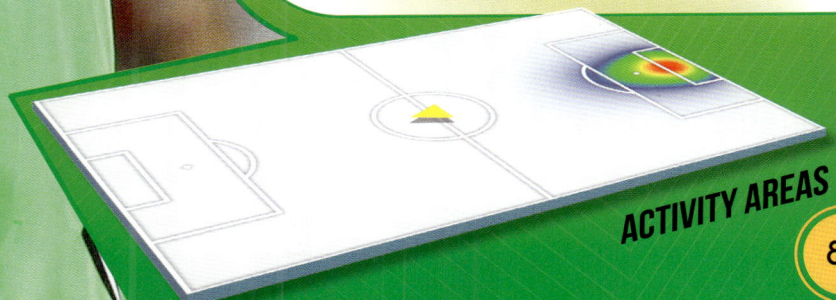

ACTIVITY AREAS

31

NATIONALITY
Brazilian

CURRENT CLUB
Manchester City

EDERSON

Owing to his range of passing and great ball skills, Ederson is often considered a playmaker goalkeeper and counted as one of the best in the English Premier League. He is a fine shot-stopper with a reputation for being a great penalty-kick saver, too.

DATE OF BIRTH	17/08/1993
POSITION	GOALKEEPER
HEIGHT	1.88 M
PRO DEBUT	2011
PREFERRED FOOT	LEFT

GOALS CONCEDED
266

APPEARANCES
330

PENALTIES SAVED
6

SAVES
593

CLEAN SHEETS
142

PENALTIES FACED
37

CATCHES
147

PUNCHES
80

MAJOR CLUB HONOURS
- ⚽ Premier League: 2018, 2019, 2021, 2022, 2023, 2024
- ⚽ UEFA Champions League: runner-up 2021, 2023
- ⚽ FA Cup: 2019, 2023, runner-up 2024

INTERNATIONAL HONOURS
- ⚽ Copa América: 2019, runner-up 2021

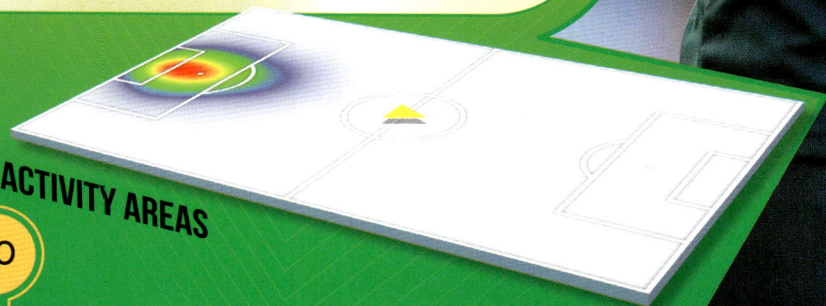

ACTIVITY AREAS

PÉTER GULÁCSI

Péter Gulácsi is dedicated to preparing for every football situation he faces. He studies approaching forwards to get an instinct for where they are going to shoot, gets into the right position and then makes difficult saves look very easy.

NATIONALITY
Hungarian

CURRENT CLUB
RB Leipzig

1

DATE OF BIRTH	06/05/1990
POSITION	GOALKEEPER
HEIGHT	1.91 M
PRO DEBUT	2008
PREFERRED FOOT	RIGHT

GOALS CONCEDED
348

APPEARANCES
295

PENALTIES SAVED
3

SAVES
711

CLEAN SHEETS
87

PENALTIES FACED
36

PUNCHES
76

CATCHES
187

MAJOR CLUB HONOURS
- Austrian Bundesliga: 2014, 2015 (Red Bull Salzburg)
- Austrian Cup: 2014, 2015 (Red Bull Salzburg)
- DFB-Pokal: runner-up* 2019*, 2021*, 2022, 2023

INTERNATIONAL HONOURS
- FIFA U-20 World Cup: third place 2009

ACTIVITY AREAS

LUKAS HRADECKY

NATIONALITY
Finnish

CURRENT CLUB
Bayer Leverkusen

1

Like many goalkeepers, it wasn't until his thirties that Lukas Hradecky reached his peak. He is an excellent shot-stopper with plenty of confidence, decisive when dealing with crosses, and brilliant at organising his penalty area and communicating with defenders.

DATE OF BIRTH	24/11/1989
POSITION	GOALKEEPER
HEIGHT	1.92 M
PRO DEBUT	2008
PREFERRED FOOT	RIGHT

GOALS CONCEDED
426

APPEARANCES
337

PENALTIES SAVED
6

CLEAN SHEETS
95

SAVES
933

PENALTIES FACED
38

CATCHES
234

PUNCHES
124

MAJOR CLUB HONOURS
- Bundesliga: 2024
- DFB Pokal: 2018 (Eintracht Frankfurt), 2024
- UEFA Europa League: runner-up 2024

INTERNATIONAL HONOURS
- Baltic Cup: Runner-up 2012

ACTIVITY AREAS

EMILIANO MARTÍNEZ

An immensely athletic goalkeeper, Emiliano Martínez is capable of reaching shots going into the top corner with either hand. His quick feet mean he gets into good positions not only to make saves but also reduce the angle for shots.

NATIONALITY
Argentinian

CURRENT CLUB
Aston Villa

1

DATE OF BIRTH	02/09/1992
POSITION	GOALKEEPER
HEIGHT	1.95 M
PRO DEBUT	2012
PREFERRED FOOT	RIGHT

GOALS CONCEDED
285

APPEARANCES
232

PENALTIES SAVED
6

SAVES
711

CLEAN SHEETS
73

PENALTIES FACED
29

PUNCHES
36

CATCHES
286

MAJOR CLUB HONOURS
⚽ FA Cup: 2020 (Arsenal)

INTERNATIONAL HONOURS
⚽ Copa América: 2021, 2024
⚽ FIFA World Cup: 2022

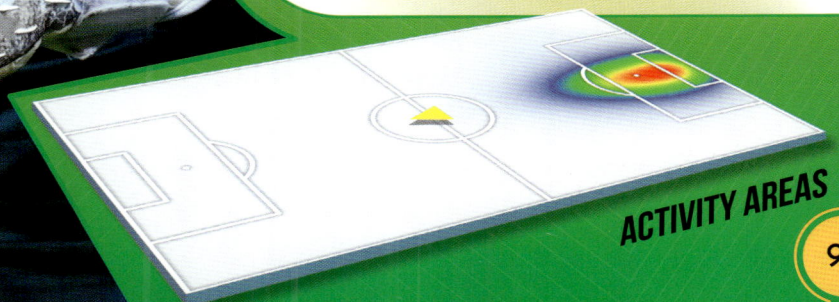

ACTIVITY AREAS

93

NATIONALITY
Costa Rican

CURRENT CLUB
TBC

KEYLOR NAVAS

Keylor Navas is strong, athletic, agile, a fine organiser and shot stopper. Part of the new breed of hyper-aggressive keepers, he has the confidence to play off his lines, even in situations that might call for more restrained positioning. Navas left French club PSG in 2024 after five years.

DATE OF BIRTH	15/12/1986
POSITION	GOALKEEPER
HEIGHT	1.85 M
PRO DEBUT	2005
PREFERRED FOOT	RIGHT

GOALS CONCEDED
310

APPEARANCES
316

PENALTIES SAVED
10

SAVES
954

CLEAN SHEETS
113

PENALTIES FACED
43

PUNCHES
135

CATCHES
164

MAJOR CLUB HONOURS

⚽ Ligue 1: 2020, '22, '24 (all PSG) ⚽ La Liga: 2017 (R. Madrid) ⚽
UEFA Champions League: 2016, '17, '18 (all R. Madrid) runner-up 2020
(PSG) ⚽ FIFA World Club Cup: 2014, '16, '17, '18 (all R. Madrid) ⚽
UEFA Super Cup: 2017 (R. Madrid) ⚽ Coupe de France: 2024 (PSG)

INTERNATIONAL HONOURS

⚽ None to date

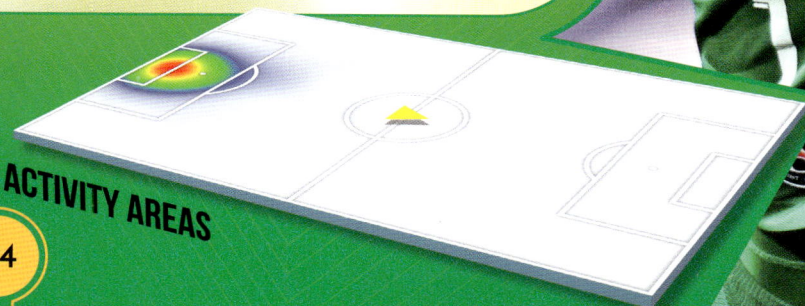

ACTIVITY AREAS

MANUEL NEUER

Manuel Neuer is famous for being football's first sweeper-keeper. He is a fine shot-stopper who commands his penalty area and marshals the defence well. He is also great with the ball at his feet, allowing defenders to play further upfield.

NATIONALITY
German

CURRENT CLUB
Bayern Munich

1

DATE OF BIRTH	27/03/1986
POSITION	GOALKEEPER
HEIGHT	1.93 M
PRO DEBUT	2004
PREFERRED FOOT	RIGHT

GOALS CONCEDED
554

APPEARANCES
641

PENALTIES SAVED
12

SAVES
1,591

CLEAN SHEETS
280

PENALTIES FACED
48

PUNCHES
276

CATCHES
603

MAJOR CLUB HONOURS

⚽ Bundesliga: 2013, '14, '15, '16, '17, '18, '19, '20, '21, '22, '23 ⚽ UEFA Champions League: 2013, 2020 ⚽ UEFA Super Cup: 2013, 2020 ⚽ FIFA Club World Cup: 2013, 2020 ⚽ DFB Pokal: 2011 (Schalke 04) 2013' '14, '16, '19, '20

INTERNATIONAL HONOURS

⚽ FIFA World Cup: 2014

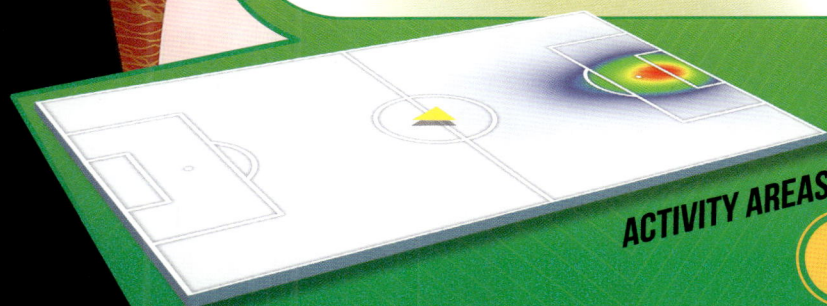

ACTIVITY AREAS

95

13

NATIONALITY
Slovenian

CURRENT CLUB
Atlético Madrid

JAN OBLAK

One of the world's most agile and accomplished keepers, Jan Oblak is blessed with the quick reflexes to be able to come off his line to snuff out any signs of danger. His communication skills make him adept at organising his defence and taking on the role of team vice-captain.

DATE OF BIRTH	07/01/1993
POSITION	GOALKEEPER
HEIGHT	1.88 M
PRO DEBUT	2009
PREFERRED FOOT	RIGHT

GOALS CONCEDED
339

APPEARANCES
427

PENALTIES SAVED
9

CLEAN SHEETS
199

SAVES
1,078

PENALTIES FACED
43

CATCHES
261

PUNCHES
121

MAJOR CLUB HONOURS
⚽ La Liga: 2021
⚽ UEFA Champions League: runner-up 2016
⚽ UEFA Europa League: 2018
⚽ UEFA Super Cup: 2018

INTERNATIONAL HONOURS
⚽ None to date

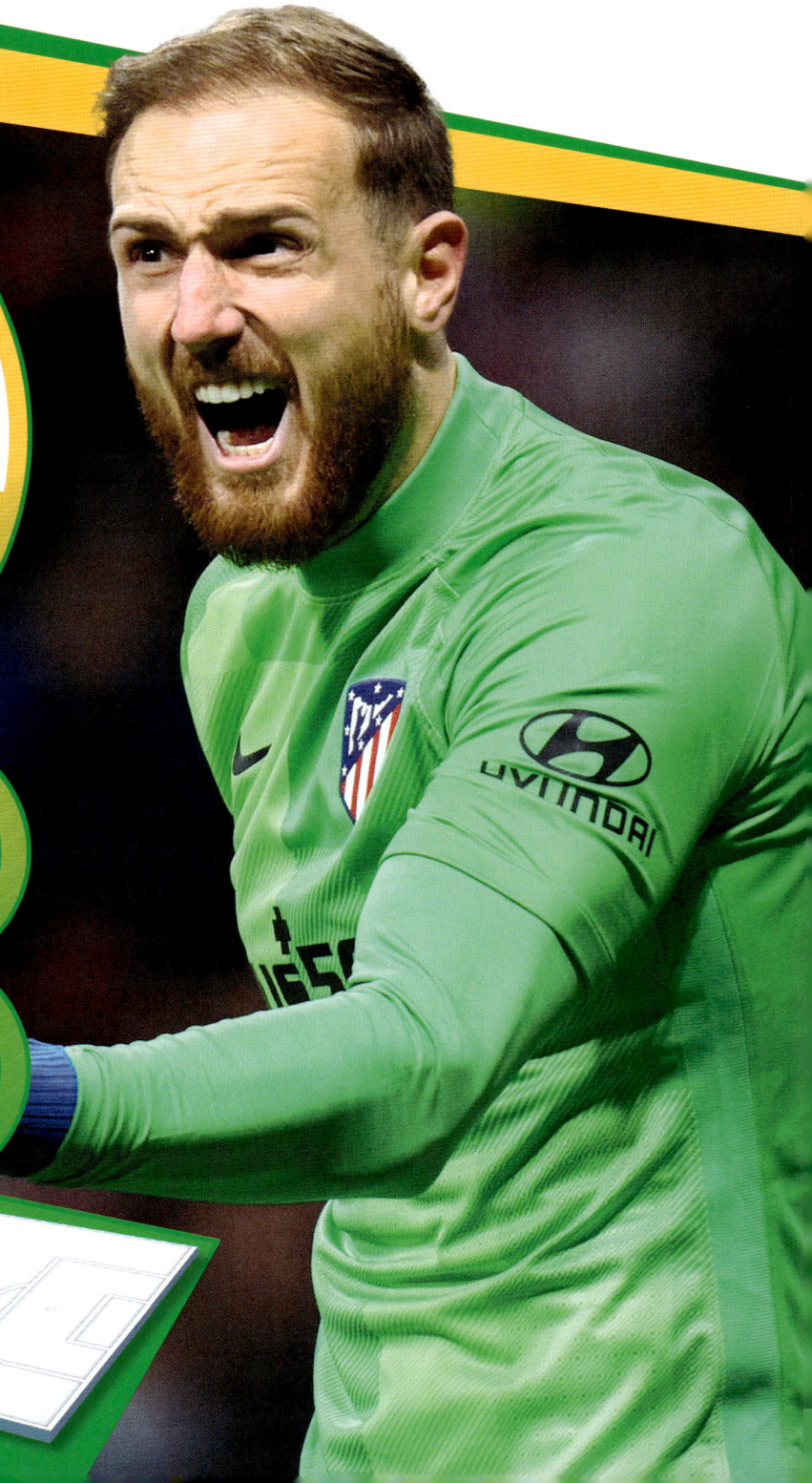

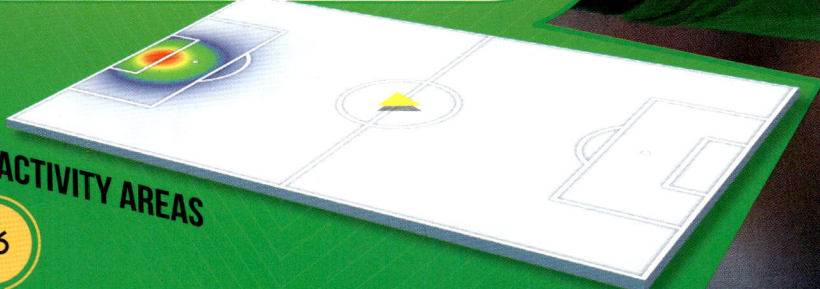

ACTIVITY AREAS

RUI PATRÍCIO

Rui Patrício is an old-fashioned continental goalkeeper, primarily a shot-stopper who allows his defenders deal with crosses into the danger area. He has great instincts and anticipation and is expert at coming off his line to narrow angles.

NATIONALITY
Portuguese

CURRENT CLUB
TBC

1

DATE OF BIRTH	15/02/1988
POSITION	GOALKEEPER
HEIGHT	1.90 M
PRO DEBUT	2006
PREFERRED FOOT	LEFT

GOALS CONCEDED
374

APPEARANCES
315

PENALTIES SAVED
6

SAVES
802

CLEAN SHEETS
98

PENALTIES FACED
36

PUNCHES
60

CATCHES
170

MAJOR CLUB HONOURS
⚽ Europa Conference League: 2022 (Roma) ⚽ Taça de Portugal: 2007, 2008, 2015 (Sporting Clube)

INTERNATIONAL HONOURS
⚽ UEFA European Championship: 2016
⚽ UEFA Nations League: 2019

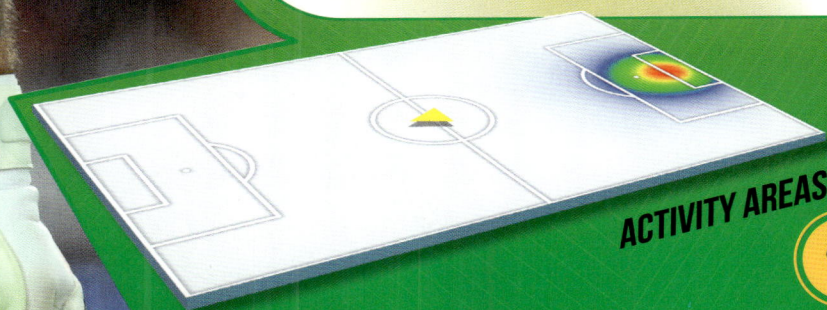

ACTIVITY AREAS

NATIONALITY
English

CURRENT CLUB
Everton

JORDAN PICKFORD

Playing for one of the lesser teams in the English Premier League, Jordan Pickford is kept busy and is an excellent shot stopper. Not the tallest of goalkeepers, he prefers to punch rather than catch the ball and is also very good at distributing to team-mates to initiate attacks.

DATE OF BIRTH	07/03/1994
POSITION	GOALKEEPER
HEIGHT	1.85 M
PRO DEBUT	2011
PREFERRED FOOT	LEFT

GOALS CONCEDED
428

APPEARANCES
289

PENALTIES SAVED
5

SAVES
918

CLEAN SHEETS
75

PENALTIES FACED
37

PUNCHES
148

CATCHES
176

MAJOR CLUB HONOURS
⚽ None to date

INTERNATIONAL HONOURS
⚽ UEFA European Championship: runner-up 2020, runner-up 2024
⚽ UEFA Natiom League: third place 2019

ACTIVITY AREAS

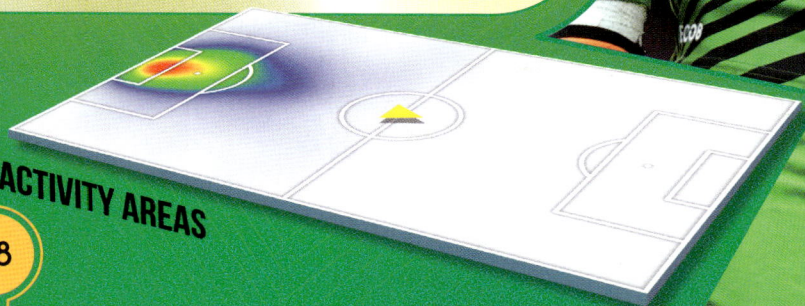

NICK POPE

Since joining The Magpies, Nick Pope has proved his worth by keeping many clean sheets for his new club. He dominates his penalty area and is excellent at stopping shots, dealing with crosses and being a sweeper-keeper outside the box.

NATIONALITY
English

CURRENT CLUB
Newcastle United

22

DATE OF BIRTH	19/04/1992
POSITION	GOALKEEPER
HEIGHT	1.91 M
PRO DEBUT	2011
PREFERRED FOOT	RIGHT

GOALS CONCEDED
222

APPEARANCES
198

PENALTIES SAVED
4

CLEAN SHEETS
66

SAVES
624

PENALTIES FACED
24

CATCHES
218

PUNCHES
89

MAJOR CLUB HONOURS
⚽ None to date

INTERNATIONAL HONOURS
⚽ None to date

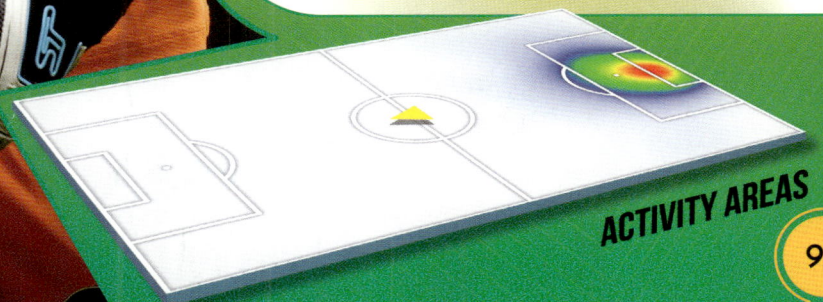

ACTIVITY AREAS

30

NATIONALITY
French

CURRENT CLUB
Lens

BRICE SAMBA

Brice Samba has the personality and physique to dominate his penalty area. His attributes include stopping shots from both long- and close-range, dealing with crosses and starting attacks with kicks downfield. He is not afraid to make unorthodox saves either.

DATE OF BIRTH	25/04/1994
POSITION	GOALKEEPER
HEIGHT	1.87 M
PRO DEBUT	2011
PREFERRED FOOT	LEFT

GOALS CONCEDED
135

APPEARANCES
121

PENALTIES SAVED
3

SAVES
393

CLEAN SHEETS
41

PENALTIES FACED
22

PUNCHES
19

CATCHES
105

MAJOR CLUB HONOURS
⚽ None to date

INTERNATIONAL HONOURS
⚽ None to date

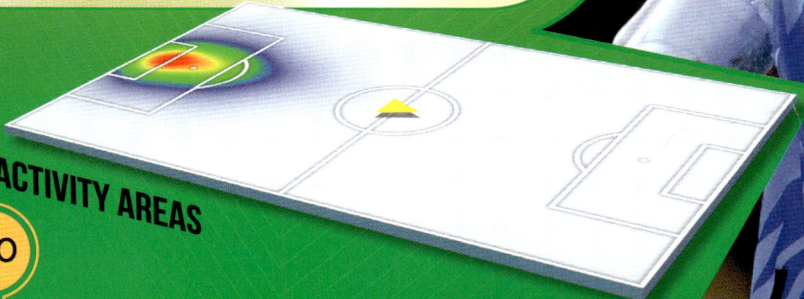

ACTIVITY AREAS

100

YANN SOMMER

Yann Sommer is not tall for a goalkeeper but he has great anticipation, reflexes and footwork which more than make up for his lack of height. A good shot-stopper, he is very comfortable playing as a sweeper-keeper, too.

NATIONALITY
Swiss

CURRENT CLUB
Inter Milan

1

DATE OF BIRTH	17/12/1988
POSITION	GOALKEEPER
HEIGHT	1.83 M
PRO DEBUT	2005
PREFERRED FOOT	LEFT

GOALS CONCEDED
529

APPEARANCES
408

PENALTIES SAVED
6

SAVES
1,330

CLEAN SHEETS
120

PENALTIES FACED
61

PUNCHES
130

CATCHES
393

MAJOR CLUB HONOURS
- Serie A: 2024
- Bundesliga: 2023 (Bayern Munich)
- Supercoppa Italiana: 2023

INTERNATIONAL HONOURS
- None to date

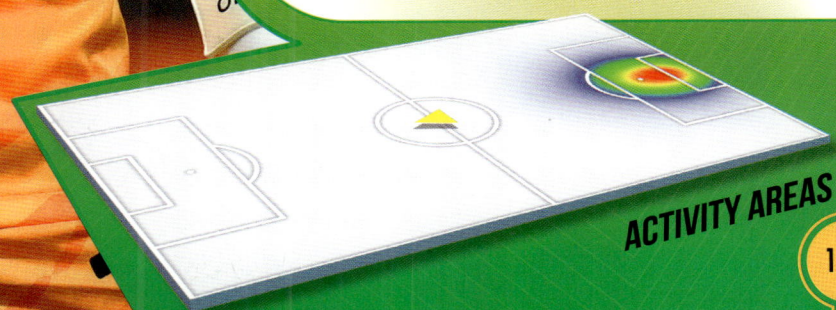

ACTIVITY AREAS

NATIONALITY
Polish

CURRENT CLUB
Juventus

WOJCIECH SZCZĘSNY

Wojciech Szczęsny has grown into one of Europe's top-class keepers. A natural shot-stopper with lightning reflexes, he is also great at controlling his penalty area, dealing with crosses and setting up counter-attacks with quick clearances.

DATE OF BIRTH	18/04/1990
POSITION	GOALKEEPER
HEIGHT	1.95 M
PRO DEBUT	2009
PREFERRED FOOT	RIGHT

GOALS CONCEDED
497

APPEARANCES
480

PENALTIES SAVED
16

CLEAN SHEETS
173

SAVES
1,258

PENALTIES FACED
77

CATCHES
391

PUNCHES
190

MAJOR CLUB HONOURS

⚽ Serie A: 2018, 2019, 2020 ⚽ FA Cup: 2014, 2015 (all Arsenal) ⚽ Coppa Italia: 2018, 2021, 2024 ⚽ Supercoppa Italiana: 2018, 2020

INTERNATIONAL HONOURS

⚽ None to date

ACTIVITY AREAS

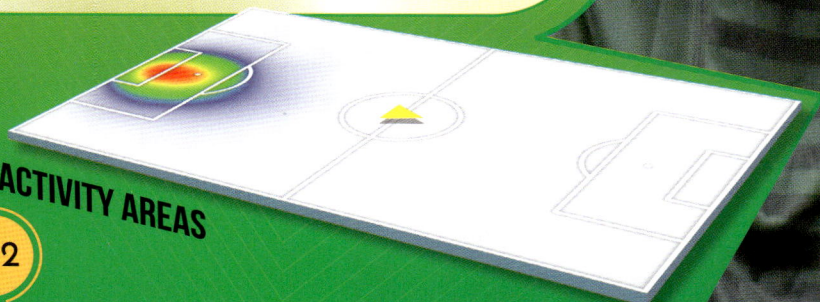

MARC-ANDRÉ TER STEGEN

A brilliant sweeper-keeper, Marc-André ter Stegen is simply world class. In addition to his fine goalkeeping qualities, he is exceptional at anticipating opponents who have beaten the offside trap, and can rush off his line to meet the danger.

NATIONALITY
German

CURRENT CLUB
Barcelona

1

DATE OF BIRTH	30/04/1992
POSITION	GOALKEEPER
HEIGHT	1.87 M
PRO DEBUT	2009
PREFERRED FOOT	RIGHT

GOALS CONCEDED
484

APPEARANCES
490

PENALTIES SAVED
7

CLEAN SHEETS
199

SAVES
1,360

PENALTIES FACED
49

CATCHES
473

PUNCHES
203

MAJOR CLUB HONOURS
⚽ La Liga: 2015, 2016, 2018, 2019, 2023 ⚽ UEFA Champions League: 2015 ⚽ UEFA Super Cup: 2015 ⚽ FIFA Club World Cup: 2015 ⚽ Copa del Rey: 2015, 2016, 2017, 2018, 2021

INTERNATIONAL HONOURS
⚽ FIFA Confederations Cup: 2017

ACTIVITY AREAS

MANAGERS

Head coaches are as different to each other as players who play in different positions. But the majority of the 12 featured in this section have one thing in common: they are all winners, either in their domestic leagues or in continental competitions. Some, such as Mikel Arteta (opposite), were successful players themselves and trophy winners well before they entered management, while others, such as Claudio Ranieri, had less fruitful playing careers but have had great success as the brains behind a top side.

WHAT DO THE STATS MEAN?

GAMES MANAGED
This is the number of matches the coach has been in charge of across their entire career in football management.

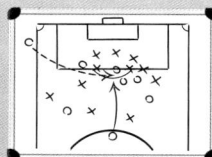

TEAMS MANAGED
The number of clubs (first teams only) that the coach has managed during their career to date.

WINS
This is the number of games the coach has won, including one leg of a cup-tie, even if the tie was lost on aggregate or penalties.

TROPHIES
The trophy list features the head coach's success in domestic top divisions, national and league cups and international club competitions, except any super cups.

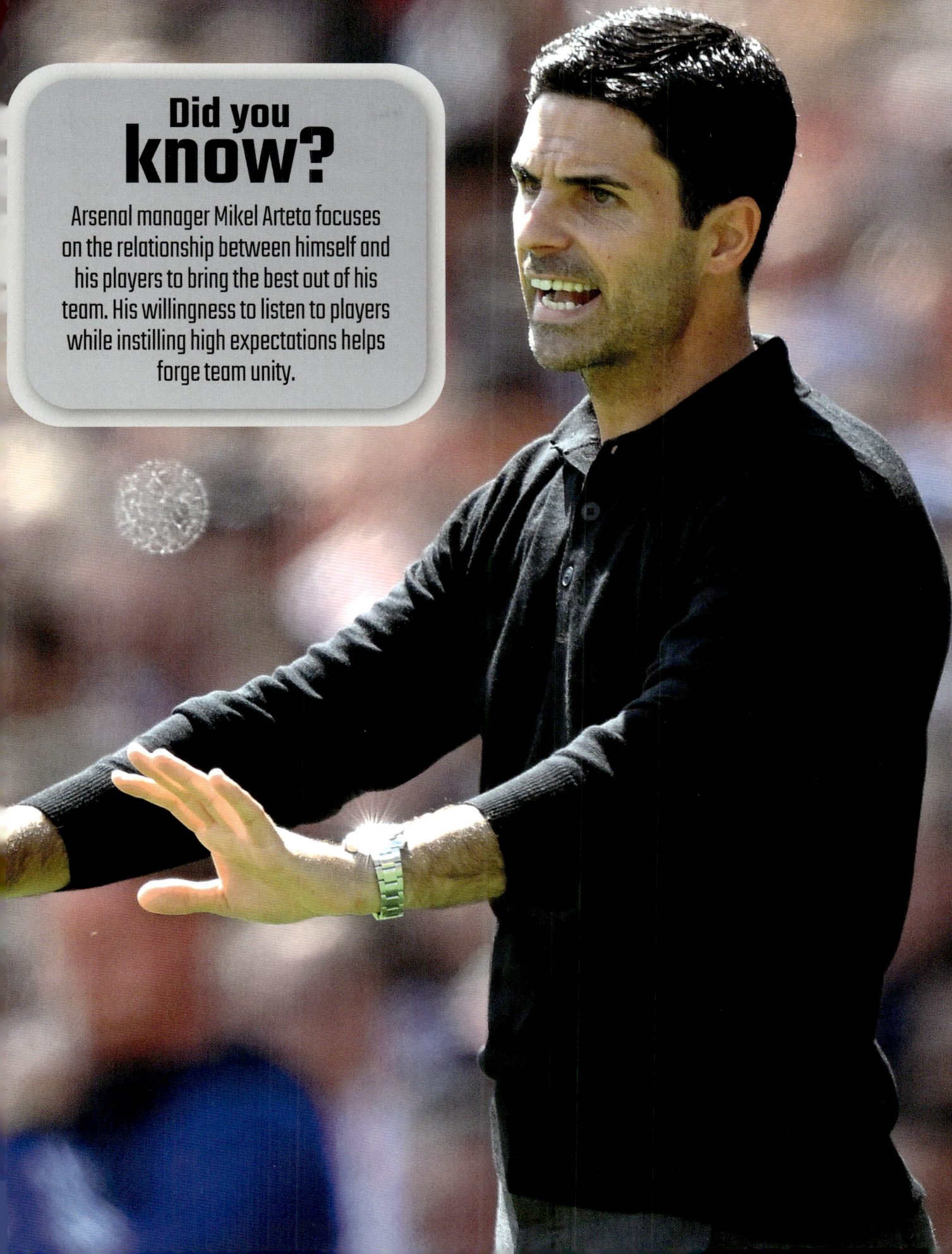

XABI ALONSO

Xabi Alonso is Europe's most in-demand coach after winning the Bundesliga title in his first full season. His teams play 3—4—2—1 formation, inviting pressure, then counter-attacking and taking advantage of holes in the opposition's defences.

NATIONALITY
Spanish

CURRENT CLUB
Bayer Leverkusen

YEARS AS HEAD COACH: 5

FIRST CLUB: REAL SOCIEDAD B

CLUBS MANAGED	GAMES	LEAGUE TITLES
2	187	1

WINS	DRAW	LOSSES
99	42	46

CHAMPIONS LEAGUE TROPHIES	EUROPA LEAGUE TROPHIES	OTHER TROPHIES*
0	0	1

MAJOR CLUB HONOURS
- ⚽ Bundesliga: 2024
- ⚽ DFB-Pokal: 2024
- ⚽ UEFA Europa League: runner-up 2024

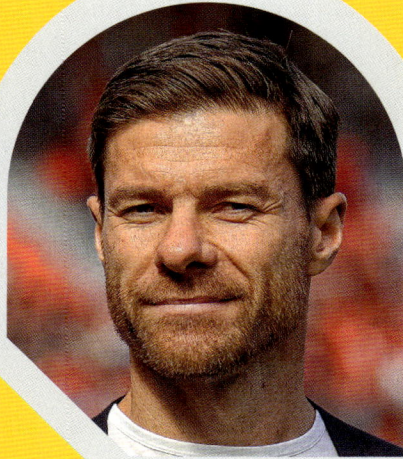

*Excludes Super Cups

CARLO ANCELOTTI

The vastly experienced and accomplished Carlo Ancelotti uses different systems depending on the opposition and players available. His favourite formation is 4—4—2, sometimes in a diamond, other times with four midfielders in a line across the pitch.

NATIONALITY
Italian

CURRENT CLUB
Real Madrid

YEARS AS HEAD COACH : 29

FIRST CLUB: REGGIANA

CLUBS MANAGED	GAMES	LEAGUE TITLES
10	1,339	6

WINS	DRAW	LOSSES
797	299	243

CHAMPIONS LEAGUE TROPHIES	EUROPA LEAGUE TROPHIES	OTHER TROPHIES*
5	0	10

MAJOR CLUB HONOURS
- ⚽ La Liga: 2022, runner-up 2023, 2024
- ⚽ UEFA Champions League: 2003, 2007 (all AC Milan), 2014, 2022, 2024
- ⚽ FIFA Club World Cup: 2007 (AC Milan), 2014, 2022
- ⚽ Serie A: 2004 (AC Milan)
- ⚽ Premier League: 2010 (Chelsea)
- ⚽ Ligue 1: 2013 (Paris St-Germain)
- ⚽ Copa del Rey: 2014, 2023
- ⚽ Bundesliga: 2017 (Bayern Munich)

*Excludes Super Cups

MIKEL ARTETA

Mikel Arteta gambled on taking a high-profile club as his first job in management. He changed his style from a defensively strong 5—4—1 to a more aggressive attacking 4—2—3—1, with players causing danger from anywhere on the pitch.

NATIONALITY
Spanish

CURRENT CLUB
Arsenal

YEARS AS HEAD COACH: 05

FIRST CLUB: ARSENAL

CLUBS MANAGED	GAMES	LEAGUE TITLES
1	232	0

WINS	DRAW	LOSSES
137	38	57

CHAMPIONS LEAGUE TROPHIES	EUROPA LEAGUE TROPHIES	OTHER TROPHIES*
0	0	3

*Excludes Super Cups

MAJOR CLUB HONOURS
- ⚽ Premier League: runner-up 2023, runner-up 2024
- ⚽ FA Cup: 2020
- ⚽ FA Community Shield: 2020, 2023

UNAI EMERY

Unai Emery has enjoyed great success managing clubs that have a modest budget. His preference is either a 4—2—3—1 formation or 4—4—2, the choice dependent on the attacking skills of the two central midfielders and their ability to retain possession.

NATIONALITY
Spanish

CURRENT CLUB
Aston Villa

YEARS AS HEAD COACH: 20

FIRST CLUB: LORCA DEPORTIVA

CLUBS MANAGED	GAMES	LEAGUE TITLES
9	1,009	1

WINS	DRAW	LOSSES
537	221	251

CHAMPIONS LEAGUE TROPHIES	EUROPA LEAGUE TROPHIES	OTHER TROPHIES*
0	4	6

*Excludes Super Cups

MAJOR CLUB HONOURS
- ⚽ UEFA Europa League: 2014, 2015, 2016 (all Sevilla), 2021 (Villareal), runner-up 2019 (Arsenal)
- ⚽ Ligue 1: 2018 (Paris Saint-Germain)
- ⚽ Coupe de France: 2017, 2018 (all Paris Saint-Germain)

LUIS ENRIQUE

Luis Enrique will not compromise his football beliefs, and he will play in the formation that suits his available players, normally 4—3—3 or 3—4—3. He wants his players to express themselves on the ball whenever possible.

NATIONALITY
Spanish

CURRENT CLUB
Paris Saint-Germain

YEARS AS HEAD COACH: 13

FIRST CLUB: BARCELONA B

CLUBS MANAGED	GAMES	LEAGUE TITLES
5	440	3

WINS	DRAW	LOSSES
263	90	87

CHAMPIONS LEAGUE TROPHIES	EUROPA LEAGUE TROPHIES	OTHER TROPHIES*
1	0	6

MAJOR CLUB HONOURS
- ⚽ UEFA Champions League; 2015 (Barcelona)
- ⚽ Ligue 1: 2024
- ⚽ La Liga; 2015, 2016 (Barcelona)
- ⚽ FIFA World Club Cup; 2015 (Barcelona)
- ⚽ Copa del Rey; 2015, 2016, 2017 (Barcelona)

*Excludes Super Cups

GIAN PIERO GASPERINI

Gian Piero Gasperini wants his teams to be attacking, but to defend man-for-man when not in possession. His 3—4—3 formation is fluid; when his teams attack, the wing-backs play as wide midfielders and try to outnumber opposing defenders.

NATIONALITY
Italian

CURRENT CLUB
Atalanta

YEARS AS HEAD COACH: 22

FIRST CLUB: CROTONE

CLUBS MANAGED	GAMES	LEAGUE TITLES
5	822	0

WINS	DRAW	LOSSES
375	198	249

CHAMPIONS LEAGUE TROPHIES	EUROPA LEAGUE TROPHIES	OTHER TROPHIES*
0	1	0

MAJOR CLUB HONOURS
- ⚽ UEFA Europa League: 2024

*Excludes Super Cups

PEP GUARDIOLA

Once a great midfielder himself, Pep Guardiola devised the *tika-taka* passing system at Barcelona (2008—12). Disciplined in possession, without the ball his teams press the opposition into making mistakes and then launch rapid counter-attacks.

NATIONALITY
Spanish

CURRENT CLUB
Manchester City

YEARS AS HEAD COACH: 17

FIRST CLUB: BARCELONA B

CLUBS MANAGED	GAMES	LEAGUE TITLES
4	922	12

WINS	DRAW	LOSSES
671	143	108

CHAMPIONS LEAGUE TROPHIES	EUROPA LEAGUE TROPHIES	OTHER TROPHIES*
3	0	15

MAJOR CLUB HONOURS
- ⚽ Premier League: 2018, 2019, 2021, 2022, 2023, 2024
- ⚽ UEFA Champions League: 2009, 2011 Barcelona), runner-up 2021, 2023
- ⚽ FIFA Club World Cup: 2009, 2011 (Barcelona), 2013 (B. Munich)
- ⚽ La Liga: 2009, 2010, 2011 (Barcelona)
- ⚽ Bundesliga: 2014, 2015, 2016 (B. Munich)
- ⚽ FA Cup: 2019, 2023, Runner-up 2024

*Excludes Super Cups

SIMONE INZAGHI

Simone Inzaghi's teams almost always play in a 3—5—2 formation. He likes his team to keep possession with short passes, patiently waiting to strike, and encourages his central defenders to draw opponents out of position to join attacks.

NATIONALITY
Italian

CURRENT CLUB
Inter Milan

YEARS AS HEAD COACH: 9

FIRST CLUB: LAZIO

CLUBS MANAGED	GAMES	LEAGUE TITLES
2	409	1

WINS	DRAW	LOSSES
238	73	98

CHAMPIONS LEAGUE TROPHIES	EUROPA LEAGUE TROPHIES	OTHER TROPHIES*
0	0	8

MAJOR CLUB HONOURS
- ⚽ Serie A: 2024
- ⚽ UEFA Champions League: runner-up 2023
- ⚽ Coppa Italia: 2019 (Lazio), 2022, 2023

*Excludes Super Cups

STEFANO PIOLI

Stefano Pioli is superb at instilling confidence into his players. This is partly because he is flexible with his tactics and focuses on the management of the individuals, getting the best out of them on the pitch. He favours a 4—2—3—1 formation.

NATIONALITY
Italian

CURRENT CLUB
AC Milan

YEARS AS HEAD COACH: 21

FIRST CLUB: SALERNITANA

CLUBS MANAGED
13

GAMES
871

LEAGUE TITLES
1

WINS
364

DRAW
250

LOSSES
257

CHAMPIONS LEAGUE TROPHIES
0

EUROPA LEAGUE TROPHIES
0

OTHER TROPHIES*
0

*Excludes Super Cups

MAJOR CLUB HONOURS
⚽ Serie A: 2022, runner-up 2024

ANGE POSTECOGLU

Ange Postecoglou is not afraid to test himself in new environments, having coached in five different countries on three continents. A fan of a 4—2—3—1 formation, his teams play open attacking football in a style popular with supporters.

NATIONALITY
Australian

CURRENT CLUB
Tottenham Hotspur

YEARS AS HEAD COACH: 23

FIRST CLUB: SOUTH MELBOURNE

CLUBS MANAGED
8

GAMES
585

LEAGUE TITLES
7

WINS
322

DRAW
110

LOSSES
153

CHAMPIONS LEAGUE TROPHIES
0

EUROPA LEAGUE TROPHIES
0

OTHER TROPHIES*
6

*Excludes Super Cups

MAJOR CLUB HONOURS
⚽ National Soccer League Champions: 1998, 1999 (South Melbourne)
⚽ OFC Club Championship: 1999 (South Melbourne)
⚽ A-League: 2011, 2012 (Brisbane Road)
⚽ J1 League: 2019 (Yokohama F Marinos)
⚽ Scottish Premiership: 2022, 2023 (Celtic)
⚽ Scottish Cup: 2023 (Celtic)

DIEGO SIMEONE

Diego Simeone likes to use a formation which is almost a 4–2–2–2 unit, with wide midfielders playing between the two central ones and the strikers. Strong defensively, his teams are great at defending set pieces and dangerous in attack.

NATIONALITY
Argentinian

CURRENT CLUB
Atlético Madrid

YEARS AS HEAD COACH: 17

FIRST CLUB: RACING CLUB

CLUBS MANAGED	GAMES	LEAGUE TITLES
7	886	4

WINS	DRAW	LOSSES
497	204	185

CHAMPIONS LEAGUE TROPHIES	EUROPA LEAGUE TROPHIES	OTHER TROPHIES*
0	2	2

*Excludes Super Cups

MAJOR CLUB HONOURS
- ⚽ UEFA Champions League: runner-up 2014, 2016
- ⚽ UEFA Europa League: 2012, 2018
- ⚽ UEFA Super Cup: 2012, 2018
- ⚽ La Liga: 2014, 2021
- ⚽ Copa del Rey: 2013
- ⚽ Primera División Apertura 2006 (Estudiantes)
- ⚽ Primera División Clausura 2008 (Racing Club)

ARNE SLOT

Arne Slot is an astute and innovative coach. He has a reputation for developing young players and playing attractive, attacking football in a 4–3–3 formation. He sometimes operates a 4–2–3–1 line up, with two midfielders in front of the back four.

NATIONALITY
Dutch

CURRENT CLUB
Liverpool

YEARS AS HEAD COACH: 8

FIRST CLUB: SC CAMBUUR

CLUBS MANAGED	GAMES	LEAGUE TITLES
3	242	1

WINS	DRAW	LOSSES
151	51	40

CHAMPIONS LEAGUE TROPHIES	EUROPA LEAGUE TROPHIES	OTHER TROPHIES*
0	0	1

*Excludes Super Cups

MAJOR CLUB HONOURS
- ⚽ Eredivisie: 2023 (Feyenoord)
- ⚽ KNVB Cup: 2024 (Feyenoord)
- ⚽ UEFA Europa Conference 2022 (Feyenoord)

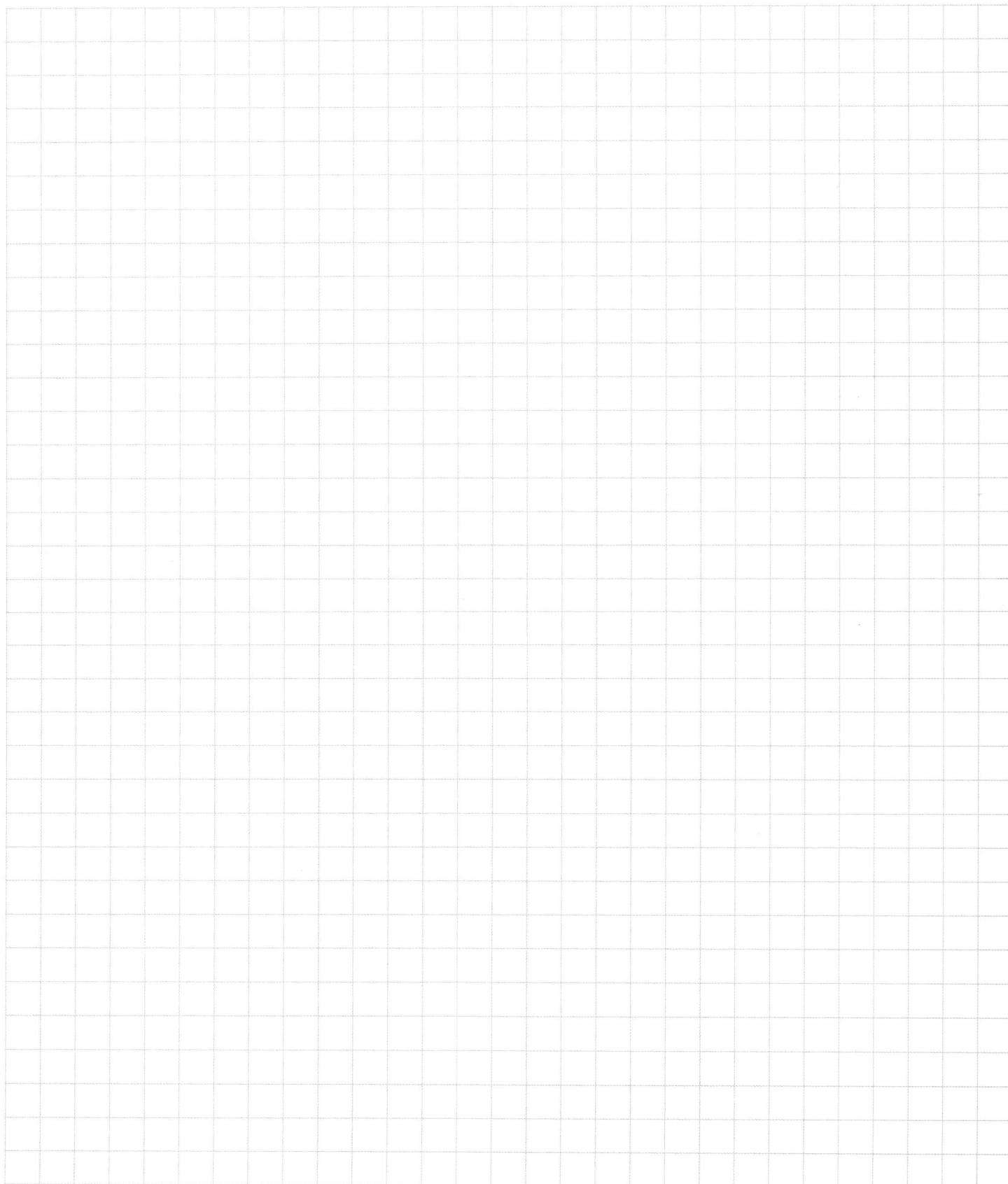

NOTES